History 1
Student Guide

Part 1

About K12 Inc.

K12 Inc., a technology-based education company, is the nation's leading provider of proprietary curriculum and online education programs to students in grades K–12. K^{12} provides its curriculum and academic services to online schools, traditional classrooms, blended school programs, and directly to families. K12 Inc. also operates the K^{12} International Academy, an accredited, diploma-granting online private school serving students worldwide. K^{12}'s mission is to provide any child the curriculum and tools to maximize success in life, regardless of geographic, financial, or demographic circumstances. K12 Inc. is accredited by CITA. More information can be found at www.K12.com.

Table of Contents

Student Worksheets and Assessments

Unit 1: Getting Around This Great Big World

Lesson 1: Getting Around the Globe 1

Lesson 2: Way to Go: Directions 9

Lesson 3: Our World: The Lay of the Land 15

Lesson 4: What Is History? 25

Lesson 5: What Is Archaeology? 29

Unit 2: Early Civilizations

Lesson 1: Nomads: Wandering Families 33

Lesson 2: Nomads Settle in the Fertile Crescent 37

Lesson 3: The First Villages 43

Lesson 4: Egyptians Lived Along the Nile River 49

Lesson 5: Gods of Ancient Egypt 58

Lesson 6: Egypt Becomes One Country (Optional) 64

Lesson 7: Hieroglyphs 73

Lesson 8: More Early Writing (Optional) 83

Lesson 9: Mummies 86

Lesson 10: The Great Pyramid 93

Lesson 11: Tutankhamen—King Tut 103

Lesson 12: The Egyptian Cinderella 111

Unit 3: The Rise of Ancient Empires

Lesson 1: Pyramids and Ziggurats 123

Lesson 2: Sargon Conquers Mesopotamia (Optional) 129

Lesson 3: Abraham Goes to Canaan 133

Lesson 4: Joseph and the Coat of Many Colors 139

Lesson 5: The Israelites Go to Egypt 144

Lesson 6: The Tower of Babel 151

Lesson 7: Hammurabi, The Fair King 156

Lesson 8: A Mesopotamian Myth: The Legend of Gilgamesh 161

Lesson 9: Rivers as Roads in Mesopotamia 167

Unit 4: Ancient Kingdoms Rise and Fall

Lesson 1: Egypt Weak and Strong (Optional)..179

Lesson 2: A Woman as Pharaoh!..186

Lesson 3: Ramses II: The Great Builder..193

Lesson 4: Moses in the Basket..201

Lesson 5: The Exodus from Egypt..213

Lesson 6: David, Israel's Second King..221

Lesson 7: Solomon, the Wise King..227

Lesson 8: The Warrior Who Built a Library (Optional)..232

Lesson 9: Back to Babylon..236

Lesson 10: Ishtar and Tammuz: A Babylonian Myth..245

Answer Keys..**253**

Student Guide
Lesson 1: Getting Around the Globe

Get to know some of the major physical features of our home, the planet Earth. Learn how historians and archaeologists interpret the human past through the lives of people and what they have left behind. Maps, globes, documents, journals, and artifacts guide the way to deeper investigation and discovery.

Lesson Objectives

- State that there are seven continents on Earth.
- Define an ocean as a large body of water.
- Name at least two major oceans.
- State that there is much more water than land on Earth.
- Define continents as the biggest pieces of land on Earth.
- Explore concepts to be addressed during the year in History 1.

PREPARE

Approximate lesson time is 60 minutes.

Advance Preparation

- It's important that you read the course introduction for Grade 1 History before you begin the first lesson. You can find it in the Help section of the Online School.
- It's important that you read the Course Introduction for History 1 before your student begins the course. You can find the course introduction at the beginning of the Getting Around the Globe lesson.

Materials

For the Student

    globe, inflatable

    ▨ Animal Picture cards

    crayons, 16 or more - assorted colors

    glue sticks

    scissors, round-end safety

    tape, clear

    map, world

    pencils, no. 2

    paper, 8 1/2" x 11"

    pencils, colored, 16 or more - assorted colors

    ▨ map of the world

    crayons, 16 or more

    paper, colored construction, 12"x12" - blue

    chalk, colored

LEARN
Activity 1: Looking at the Earth from Outer Space *(Online)*

Activity 2: Traveling the World *(Online)*

Activity 3: Continents and Oceans *(Online)*

Activity 4: Show You Know *(Online)*

Activity 5: History Record Book *(Online)*

Activity 6. Optional: What Are They and Where Are They? *(Online)*

ASSESS
Lesson Assessment: Getting Around the Globe (*Offline*)
You will complete an offline assessment covering the main objectives of this lesson. Your learning coach will score this assessment.

LEARN
Activity 7. Optional: Sidewalk World Map *(Online)*

Activity 8: Welcome to History 1 *(Online)*

Animal Picture Cards

cut

Hedgehog

Kangaroo

Panda

Toucan

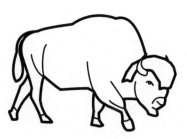

Bison

Elephant

Penguin

Giraffe

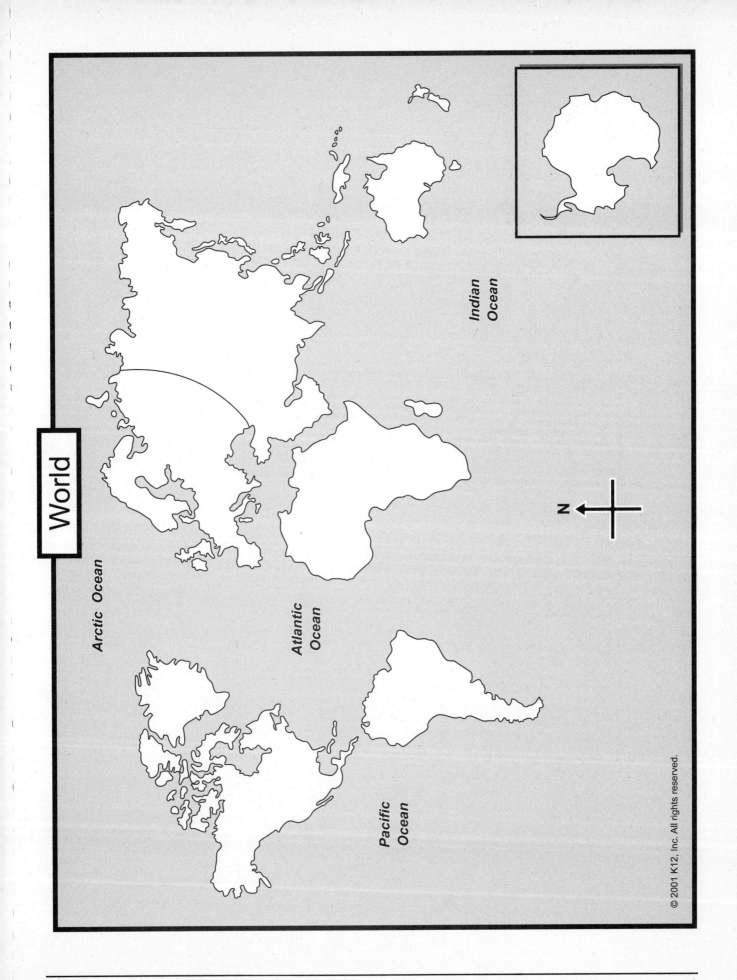

World

Arctic Ocean

Indian Ocean

Atlantic Ocean

Pacific Ocean

N

Lesson Assessment

Getting Around the Globe

Short-Answer Questions:

1. What do we call the biggest pieces of land on Earth?

2. How many continents are there?

3. What do we call the biggest bodies of water on Earth?

4. Is there more land or water on Earth?

5. Name two oceans.

Student Guide
Lesson 2: Way to Go: Directions

Lesson Objectives

- Show how to move north, south, east, and west on a map or globe.
- Identify the purpose of a compass rose.
- Identify the directions north, south, east, and west on a compass rose.
- Locate the following on a map or globe: equator, North Pole, South Pole.

PREPARE

Approximate lesson time is 60 minutes.

Materials

For the Student

>>> globe, inflatable
>>> 🖳 Compass Rose activity sheet
>>> map, world
>>> index cards, 4" x 6"
>>> tape, clear
>>> pencils, no. 2
>>> paper, 8 1/2" x 11"
>>> pencils, colored, 16 or more
>>> compass

LEARN
Activity 1: Reviewing the Continents (Online)

Activity 2: North, South, East, and West (Online)

Activity 3: The Poles and the Equator (Online)

Activity 4: Continents and Countries (Online)

Activity 5: Show You Know *(Online)*

Activity 6: History Record Book *(Online)*

Activity 7. Optional: Turn in the Right Direction *(Online)*

Activity 8. Optional: Move in the Right Direction *(Online)*

ASSESS

Lesson Assessment: Way to Go: Directions (*Offline*)

You will complete an offline assessment covering the main objectives of this lesson. Your learning coach will score this assessment.

LEARN

Activity 9. Optional: Compass Practice *(Online)*

Name _____   Date _____

Compass Rose

Write the letters *S, E,* and *W* near the corresponding points of the compass rose to indicate the directions south, east, and west.

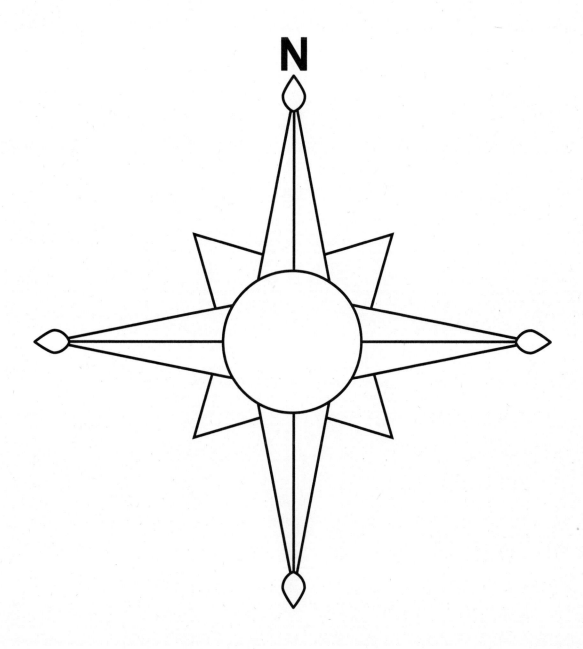

Name _____ Date _____

Lesson Assessment

Way to Go: Directions

Short-Answer Questions:

1. What is the purpose of the compass rose?

2. What are the directions on the compass rose?

3. Which direction is North?

4. Where are the North Pole, South Pole, and equator located?

Student Guide
Lesson 3: Our World: The Lay of the Land

Lesson Objectives

- Identify the following landforms from pictures: mountain, desert, canyon, island, and peninsula.
- Identify the following landforms from pictures: river, lake, and glacier.

PREPARE

Approximate lesson time is 60 minutes.

Materials

For the Student

 globe, inflatable

 map, world

 🗊 Explorer Page activity sheet

 crayons, 16 or more

 glue sticks

 scissors, round-end safety

 🗊 Anywhere Land activity sheet

 pencils, colored, 16 or more

 pencils, no. 2

 paper, 8 1/2" x 11"

 Elmer's Glue-All

 index cards, 4" x 6"

 Maps and Globes by Jack Knowlton

Keywords and Pronunciation

glacier (GLAY-shur)

Himalayan (hih-muh-LAY-uhn)

oasis (oh-AY-sis)

Sahara (suh-HAIR-uh)

LEARN
Activity 1: Question and Answer (Online)

Activity 2: World Explorer *(Online)*

Activity 3: Map Legends *(Online)*

Activity 4: Show You Know *(Online)*

Activity 5: History Record Book *(Online)*

Activity 6. Optional: Finding Photos *(Online)*

Activity 7. Optional: Flash Cards *(Online)*

ASSESS
Lesson Assessment: Our World: The Lay of the Land (*Offline*)
You will complete an offline assessment covering the main objectives of this lesson. Your learning coach will score this assessment.

LEARN
Activity 8. Optional: Maps and Globes *(Online)*

✂ cut

mountains : river : canyon : lake : desert : peninsula : island : glacier

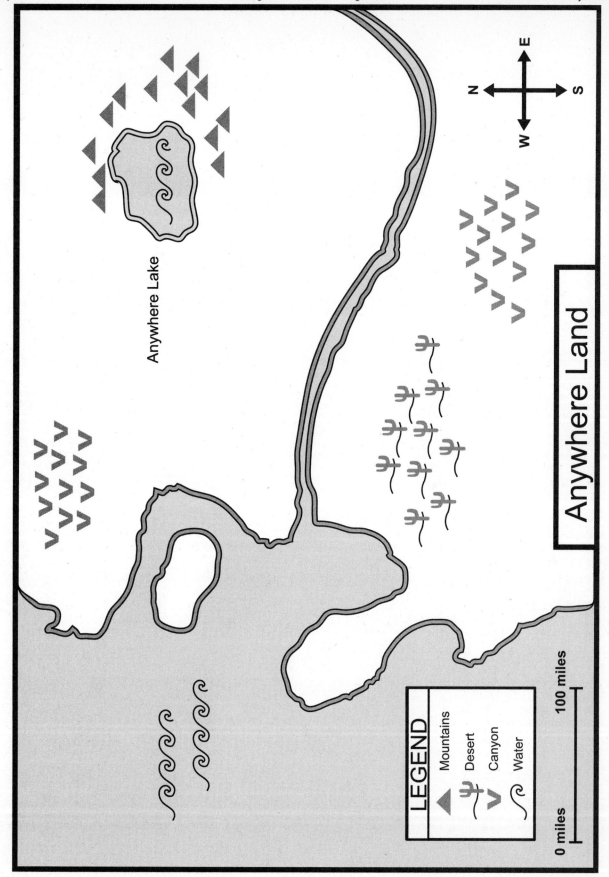

Anywhere Land

Anywhere Lake

LEGEND

Mountains

Desert

Canyon

Water

0 miles   100 miles

Lesson Assessment

Our World: The Lay of the Land

Short-Answer Questions:

1. Which image shows a glacier?

2. Which image shows a mountain?

3. Which image shows a desert?

4. Which image shows a lake?

5. Which image shows an island?

6. Which image shows a peninsula?

7. Which image shows a canyon?

8. Which image shows a river?

✂ cut

mountains ┆ river ┆ canyon ┆ lake ┆ desert ┆ peninsula ┆ island ┆ glacier

Student Guide
Lesson 4: What Is History?

Lesson Objectives

- Define history as the story of the past.
- Know that historians use pictures, letters, and other sources to learn about the past.

PREPARE

Approximate lesson time is 60 minutes.

Materials

For the Student

    globe, inflatable

    pencils, no. 2

    paper, 8 1/2" x 11"

    pencils, colored, 16 or more

    markers, colored, 8 or more

    shoeboxes

    crayons, 16 or more

    ruler, standard 12"

    tape, clear

Keywords and Pronunciation

historian : A person who studies the human past to know how people lived, what happened to them, and what they did.

history : The story of the past.

LEARN
Activity 1: Review with the Globe *(Online)*

Activity 2: Jesse and the Shoebox *(Online)*

Activity 3: Stories from the Past *(Online)*

Activity 4: Show You Know *(Online)*

Activity 5: History Record Book *(Online)*

Activity 6. Optional: Memory Box *(Online)*

Activity 7. Optional: What is History? *(Online)*

ASSESS

Lesson Assessment: What is History? *(Offline)*
You will complete an offline assessment covering the main objectives of this lesson. Your learning coach will score this assessment.

LEARN
Activity 8. Optional: Timeline *(Online)*

Lesson Assessment

What is History?

Short-Answer Questions:

1. What is the story of the past called?
2. Jesse found things that historians use to figure out the story of the past. What kind of things did he find in the shoebox?

Student Guide
Lesson 5: What Is Archaeology?

Lesson Objectives

- Demonstrate mastery of important knowledge and skills taught in this unit.
- Describe archaeology as one way of learning about the past.
- Explain that archaeologists dig up and study objects that ancient peoples left behind.
- Identify the directions north, south, east, and west on a compass rose.

PREPARE

Approximate lesson time is 60 minutes.

Materials

For the Student

marker, black permanent, non-toxic

index cards, 4" x 6"

History Record Book

Keywords and Pronunciation

archaeologist (ahr-kee-AH-luh-jist) : A person who studies the objects that ancient peoples have left behind, such as tools, pottery, buildings, bones, or jewelry.

archaeologists (ahr-kee-AH-luh-jists)

archaeology (ahr-kee-AH-luh-jee) : Study of the objects that ancient peoples have left behind, such as tools, pottery, buildings, bones or jewelry.

LEARN
Activity 1: A Look at the Past *(Online)*

Activity 2: Creating the Past *(Online)*

Activity 3: Uncovering the Past *(Online)*

Activity 4. Optional: An Archaeology Dig *(Online)*

Activity 5: Reviewing Unit One *(Online)*

ASSESS

Unit Assessment: Getting Around this Great Big World (*Offline*)

Complete an offline Unit Assessment. Your learning coach will score this part of the Assessment.

Name _____   Date _____

Geography and History Overview

Fill in the blanks with the correct answer.

1. How many continents are there on Earth? _____

2. Is there more land or water on the Earth? _____

3. Place the directions south, east, north, and west in the correct locations on the compass rose.

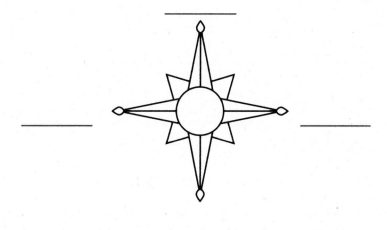

Shade or color in the bubble next to the correct answer.

4. Africa and Asia are both _____ .

    ○ islands

    ○ continents

    ○ peninsulas

5. Large bodies of water, like the Atlantic and Pacific, are _____.

    ○ oceans

    ○ lakes

    ○ rivers

6. A lake is a body of water surrounded by _____.

    ○ mountains

    ○ ice

    ○ land

7. Name a dry, sandy place where it's hard for plants and animals to live:

    ○ mountain

    ○ desert

    ○ glacier

8. Canyons look like _____.

    ○ deep cracks in the earth

    ○ big chunks of ice

    ○ small pools of water

9. The story of the human past is called _____.

    ○ geography

    ○ history

    ○ science

10. Who studies the past by digging up the objects people of the past have left behind?

    ○ archaeologists

    ○ doctors

    ○ map-makers

Student Guide
Lesson 1: Nomads: Wandering Families

Learn how civilization first developed in the Fertile Crescent, where once nomadic people settled in villages, planted crops, and domesticated animals. Their settlements eventually grew along the banks of the Nile River into the great civilization of ancient Egypt. Led by their pharaohs, the Egyptians built pyramids, tombs, and sphinxes.

Lesson Objectives

- Define a nomad as a wanderer who moves from place to place.
- Describe the foods and shelters used by nomadic peoples.
- Explain that nomads moved often to find food.

PREPARE

Approximate lesson time is 60 minutes.

Materials

For the Student

crayons, 16 or more

pencils, no. 2

paper, 8 1/2" x 11"

chalk, colored

Living in Prehistoric Times by Jane Chisholm

Who Were the First People? by Phil Cox, et. al.

It's Disgusting-And We Ate It! by James Solheim

Keywords and Pronunciation

herd : A group of animals.

nomad : A wanderer who moves from place to place.

LEARN
Activity 1: Home Is Where You Lay Your Head (Online)

Activity 2: Nomads: Families Long Ago (Online)

Activity 3: The Story of Tarak, Part 1 *(Online)*

Activity 4: Show You Know *(Online)*

Activity 5: History Record Book *(Online)*

Activity 6. Optional: Nature Walk *(Online)*

Activity 7. Optional: Cave Paintings *(Online)*

ASSESS

Lesson Assessment: Nomads: Wandering Families (*Offline*)

You will complete an offline assessment covering the main objectives of this lesson. Your learning coach will score this assessment.

LEARN

Activity 8. Optional: More About Nomads *(Online)*

Activity 9. Optional: More Incredible Edibles *(Online)*

Lesson Assessment

Nomads: Wandering Families

Short-Answer Questions:

1. What were the nomads?

2. What kinds of growing things did the nomads eat?

3. What kinds of large animals did they eat?

4. Why did nomads move from place to place?

5. Where did the nomads sleep?

Student Guide
Lesson 2: Nomads Settle in the Fertile Crescent

Lesson Objectives

- Explain that nomads settled in places where there was plenty of food and water.
- Identify the Fertile Crescent as an area where nomads settled.

PREPARE

Approximate lesson time is 60 minutes.

Materials

For the Student

    🖥 map of the Fertile Crescent

    crayons, 16 or more

    map, world

    🖥 Show You Know

    pencils, no. 2

    paper, 8 1/2" x 11"

    paper, colored construction, 12"x12"

    tape recorder

    cardboard, sheets

    Legos

    Play-Doh

    shoeboxes

    Living in Prehistoric Times by Jane Chisholm

    Who Were the First People? by Phil Cox, et. al.

Keywords and Pronunciation

Euphrates (yoo-FRAY-teez)

Fertile Crescent : An area of rich land located between the Tigris and Euphrates Rivers and extending along the Nile River.

Mediterranean (med-uh-tuh-RAY-nee-uhn)

Mesopotamia (meh-suh-puh-TAY-mee-uh) : Means "land between rivers."

nomad : A wanderer who moves from place to place.

Tigris (TIY-gruhs)

LEARN
Activity 1: Finding Food for Nomads *(Online)*

Activity 2: The Story of Tarak, Part 2 *(Online)*

Activity 3: Find the Fertile Crescent *(Online)*

Activity 4: Show You Know *(Online)*

Activity 5: History Record Book *(Online)*

Activity 6. Optional: Tarak's Journal *(Online)*

Activity 7. Optional: Tarak's New Home *(Online)*

ASSESS
Lesson Assessment: Nomads Settle in the Fertile Crescent (*Offline*)
You will complete an offline assessment covering the main objectives of this lesson. Your learning coach will score this assessment.

LEARN
Activity 8. Optional: More About People Long Ago *(Online)*

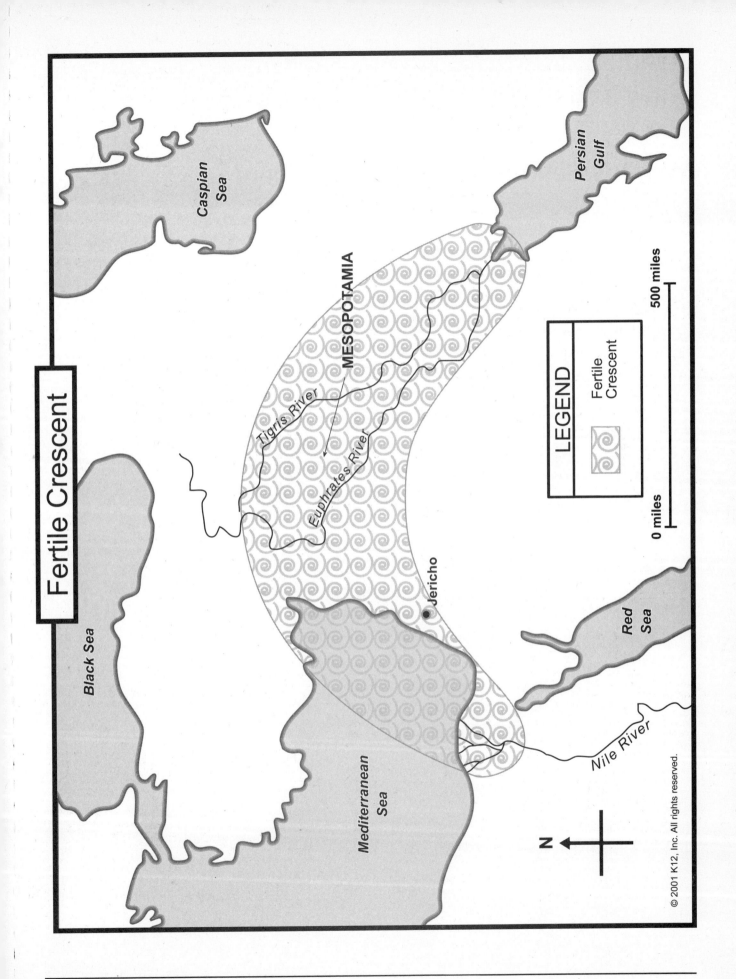

Fertile Crescent

Caspian Sea

Persian Gulf

MESOPOTAMIA

Tigris River

Euphrates River

Black Sea

Jericho

LEGEND

Fertile Crescent

0 miles

500 miles

Mediterranean Sea

Red Sea

Nile River

N

© 2001 K12, Inc. All rights reserved.

Show You Know

Nomads Settle in the Fertile Crescent

Short-Answer Questions:

1. What do we call the area where many nomad families settled?

2. The nomads settled in the Fertile Crescent because they found some things there that they needed to live. What very important things did nomads find in the Fertile Crescent?

Lesson Assessment

Nomads Settle in the Fertile Crescent

Short-Answer Questions:

1. What do we call the area where many nomad families settled?

2. The nomads settled in the Fertile Crescent because they found some things there that they needed to live. What very important things did nomads find in the Fertile Crescent?

Student Guide
Lesson 3: The First Villages

Lesson Objectives

- Identify early farmers as settlers of the first villages.
- Explain that in Mesopotamia and other regions farmers needed to irrigate, or transport, water to help their crops grow.
- Explain that farmers tamed cows, goats, and other animals so they wouldn't have to rely on hunting for meat.

PREPARE

Approximate lesson time is 60 minutes.

Materials

For the Student

🖳 map of the Fertile Crescent

crayons, 16 or more

pencils, no. 2

paper, 8 1/2" x 11"

pencils, colored, 16 or more

flour

foil, aluminum

bowl

cookie sheet

water

cardboard, sheets

clay, colored

figurines, animal

figurines, people

pebbles

toy boat

twigs - small

markers, colored, 8 or more

God's People: Stories from the Old Testament, retold by Geraldine McCaughrean

Keywords and Pronunciation

domesticated : Trained to live with or be useful to humans.

irrigate : To supply water by means of streams, ditches, or pipes.

Jericho (JER-ih-koh)

Mesopotamia (meh-suh-puh-TAY-mee-uh) : Means "land between rivers."

shaduf (shuh-DOOF) : Early farming machine that helped farmers bring water to their crops from canals or other sources.

LEARN
Activity 1: A Good Place for a Village (Online)

Activity 2: Begin with Farming (Online)

Activity 3: The Walled City: Jericho (Online)

Activity 4: Show You Know (Online)

Activity 5: History Record Book (Online)

Activity 6. Optional: Make Mud Bricks (Online)

Activity 7. Optional: Model of an Ancient Village (Online)

ASSESS

Lesson Assessment: The First Villages (Offline)

You will complete an offline assessment covering the main objectives of this lesson. Your learning coach will score this assessment.

LEARN
Activity 8. Optional: More About Jericho (Online)

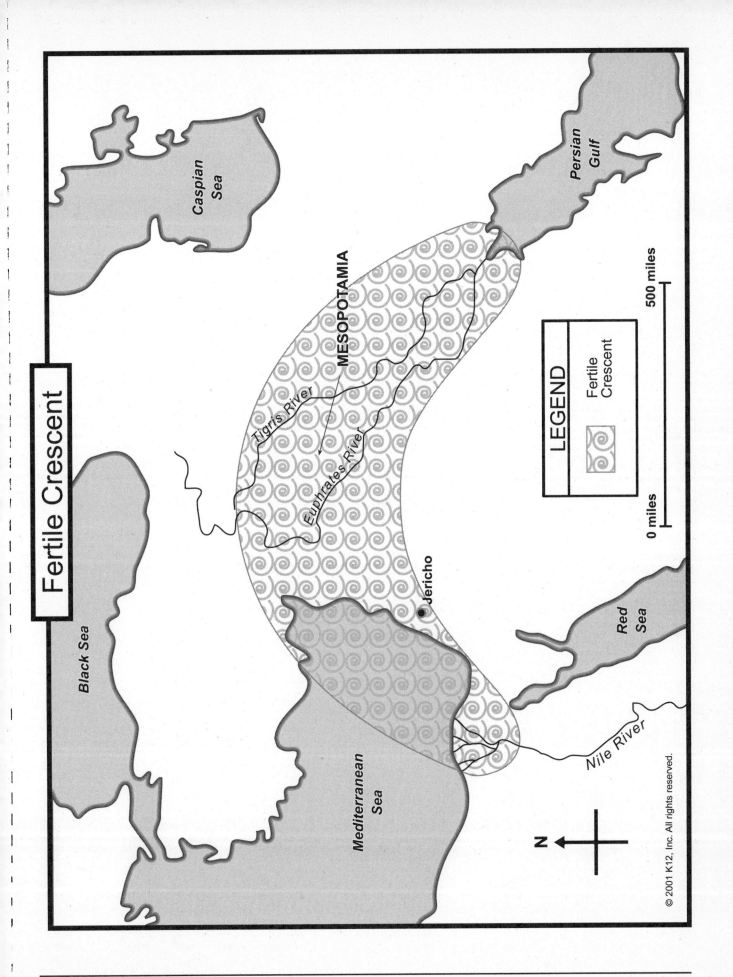

Fertile Crescent

MESOPOTAMIA

Caspian Sea

Persian Gulf

Tigris River

Euphrates River

Jericho

Black Sea

Mediterranean Sea

Red Sea

Nile River

LEGEND

Fertile Crescent

0 miles   500 miles

N

© 2001 K12, Inc. All rights reserved.

Lesson Assessment

The First Villages

Short-Answer Questions:

1. Who settled the first villages?

2. How did farmers in Mesopotamia water their crops?

3. Why didn't farmers have to hunt wild animals?

Student Guide
Lesson 4: Egyptians Lived Along the Nile River

Lesson Objectives

- Recall that regular flooding of the Nile leaves behind good soil for farming.
- Find the Nile River on a map.
- Locate the Egyptian empire along the Nile River.

PREPARE

Approximate lesson time is 60 minutes.

Materials

For the Student

- 🖳 map of the Fertile Crescent
- 🖳 map of the Nile River Valley
- globe, inflatable
- map, world - current
- crayons, 16 or more
- pencils, no. 2
- paper, 8 1/2" x 11"
- clay, colored
- pan, baking
- sand, dry
- soil, potting
- spatula
- water
- 🖳 Nile River Farming Picture
- markers, colored, 8 or more
- Bill and Pete Go Down the Nile by Tomie dePaola

Keywords and Pronunciation

delta : A gathering of sand, mud, and earth at the mouth of a river.

Egypt : A country in northeast Africa bordering on the Mediterranean and Red Seas.

flooding : The overflowing of water onto dry land.

Nile River : The longest river in the world; the Nile runs through east Africa from Lake Victoria to northern Egypt and the Mediterranean Sea.

silt : Small pieces of sand and clay washed up from the bottom of a river.

LEARN
Activity 1: Remember the Nomads *(Online)*

Activity 2: The Importance of Water *(Online)*

Activity 3: Where Is the Nile River? *(Online)*

Activity 4: Show You Know *(Online)*

Activity 5: History Record Book *(Online)*

Activity 6. Optional: Make a Model *(Online)*

Activity 7. Optional: Picture This--Egyptian Farmers *(Online)*

ASSESS

Lesson Assessment: Egyptians Lived Along the Nile River (*Offline*)

You will complete an offline assessment covering the main objectives of this lesson. Your learning coach will score this assessment.

LEARN
Activity 8. Optional: Read More! *(Online)*

Activity 9. Optional: The Nile Today *(Online)*

Fertile Crescent

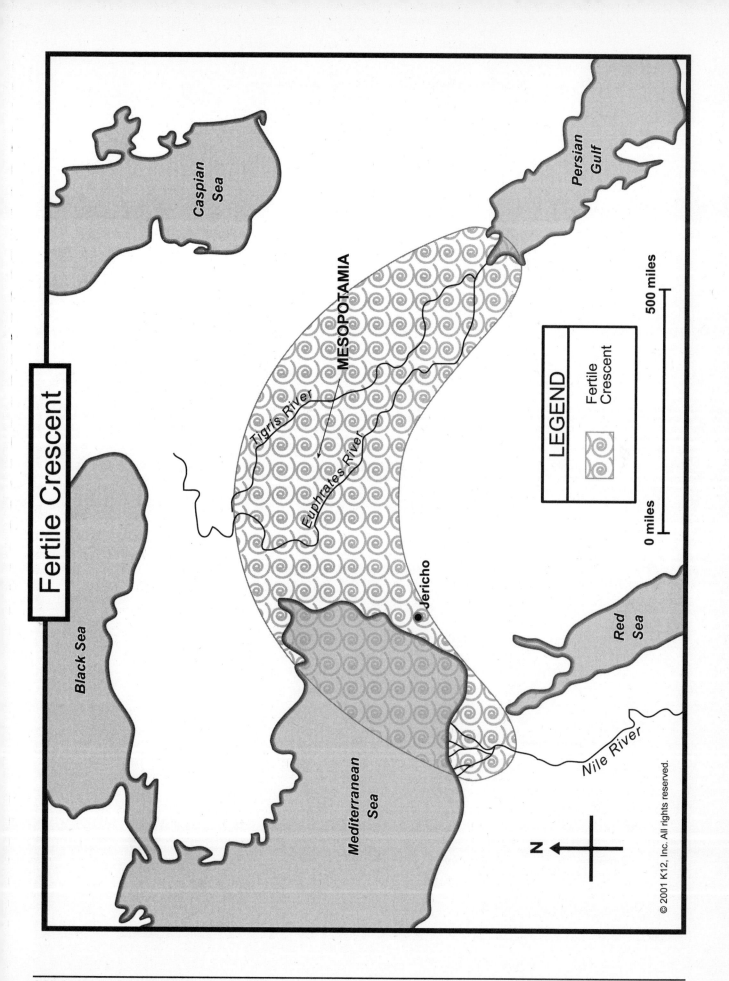

LEGEND

Fertile Crescent

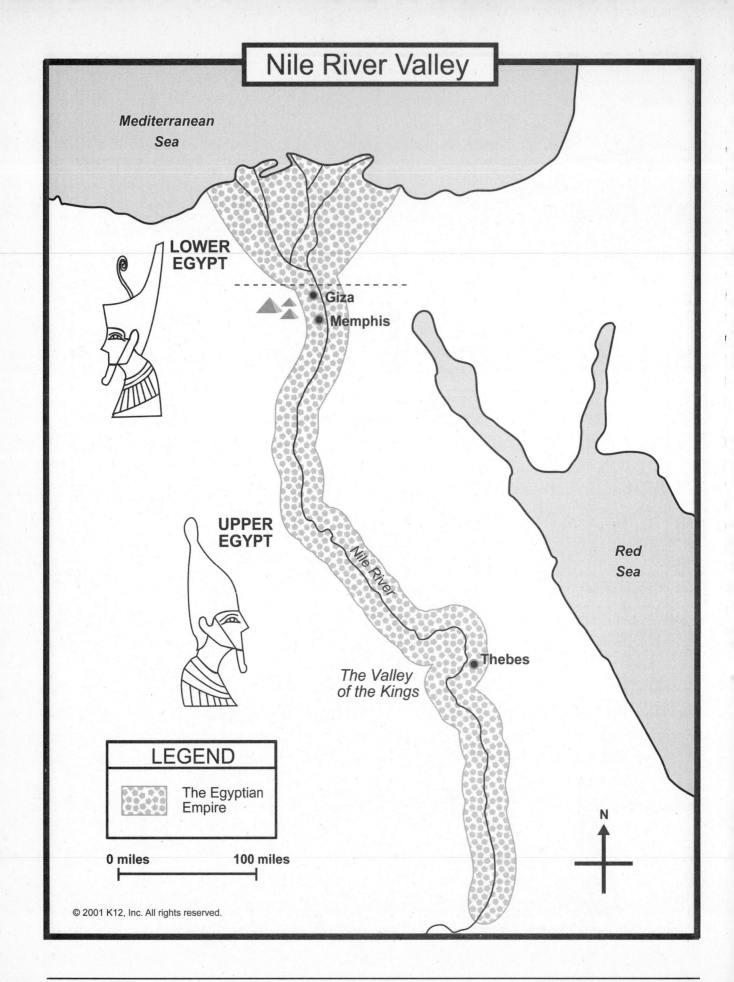

Nile River Valley

Mediterranean
Sea

**LOWER
EGYPT**

Giza

Memphis

**UPPER
EGYPT**

Nile River

Red
Sea

Thebes

*The Valley
of the Kings*

LEGEND

The Egyptian
Empire

0 miles   100 miles

N

52

53

Lesson Assessment

Egyptians Lived Along the Nile River

To answer these questions, please use your map of Nile River Valley:

1. Where is the Nile River located?

2. Where was the Egyptian empire located?

3. What does the regular flooding of the Nile leave behind?

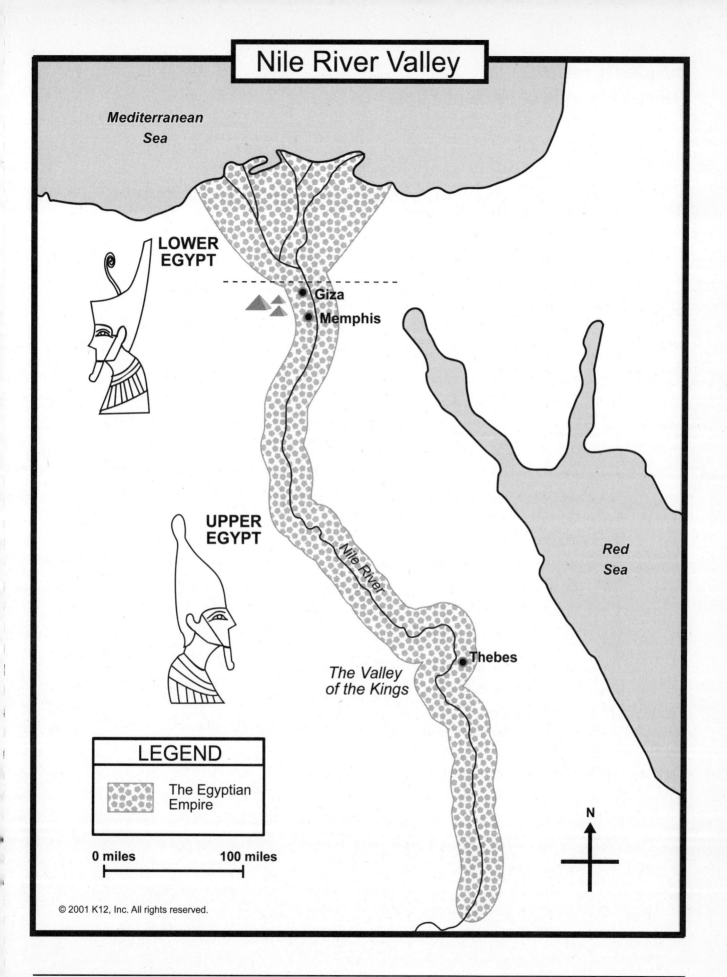

Nile River Valley

Mediterranean Sea

LOWER EGYPT

Giza

Memphis

UPPER EGYPT

Nile River

Red Sea

Thebes

The Valley of the Kings

LEGEND

The Egyptian Empire

0 miles — 100 miles

N

Student Guide
Lesson 5: Gods of Ancient Egypt

Lesson Objectives

- Know that the ancient Egyptians worshipped many gods.
- Explain that Egyptians thought the gods controlled nature (such as the sun, the rain, the Nile River).
- Identify Amun-Ra as the sun god.
- Identify Osiris as the god of the Nile.

PREPARE

Approximate lesson time is 60 minutes.

Materials

For the Student

    🖳 map of the Nile River Valley

    crayons, 16 or more

    pencils, no. 2

    paper, 8 1/2" x 11"

    🖳 Isis and Osiris activity sheet

    markers, colored, 8 or more

    pencils, colored, 16 or more

    foil, aluminum

    paint, gold

    paper, colored construction, 12"x12"

    Elmer's Glue-All

    glitter

    The Gods and Goddesses of Ancient Egypt by Leonard Everett Fisher

    Egyptian Treasures: Mummies and Myths by Jim Weiss

Keywords and Pronunciation

Amun-Ra (ah-muhn-RAH) : Egyptian god of the sun

Isis (IY-suhs) : wife of Osiris

Osiris (oh-SIY-ruhs) : Egyptian god of the Nile River

LEARN
Activity 1: Nile Review *(Online)*

Activity 2: Egyptian Religion *(Online)*

Activity 3: Show You Know *(Online)*

Activity 4: History Record Book *(Online)*

Activity 5. Optional: Egyptian Art *(Online)*

Activity 6. Optional: Amun-Ra and his Sky Boat *(Online)*

ASSESS
Lesson Assessment: Gods of Ancient Egypt (*Offline*)
You will complete an offline assessment covering the main objectives of this lesson. Your learning coach will score this assessment.

LEARN
Activity 7. Optional: Egyptian Myths *(Online)*

Activity 8. Optional: Egyptian Storytelling *(Online)*

Lesson Assessment

Gods of Ancient Egypt

Short-Answer Questions:

1. Did the ancient Egyptians believe in just one god or many gods?

2. Who did the Egyptians think caused the floods?

3. What part of nature did Amun-Ra control?

4. Who was the Egyptian god of the Nile?

Student Guide
Lesson 6. Optional: Egypt Becomes One Country

Lesson Objectives

- State that Egypt was once divided into two parts: Upper Egypt and Lower Egypt.
- Locate Upper Egypt and Lower Egypt on a map.
- Identify the Double Crown of Egypt.

PREPARE

Approximate lesson time is 60 minutes.

Materials

For the Student

     📖 map of the Nile River Valley

     crayons, 16 or more

     History Record Book

     pencils, no. 2

     paper, 8 1/2" x 11"

     pencils, colored, 16 or more

     📖 Red Crown pattern sheet

     📖 White Crown cut-out sheet

     glue sticks

     paper, colored construction, 12"x12"

     scissors, round-end safety

     📖 King Narmer picture

     The Egyptian Cinderella by Shirley Climo (ISBN 0064432793)

Keywords and Pronunciation

Lower Egyptians : Egyptians who lived on the downstream part of the Nile River, close to the Mediterranean Sea.

Menes (MEE-neez)

Narmer (NAHR-mur) : The name of the pharaoh, or king, who united Upper Egypt and Lower Egypt.

Pharaoh (FAIR-oh) : an Egyptian king

Upper Egyptians : Egyptians who lived on the upstream part of the Nile River, farther from the Mediterranean Sea.

LEARN
Activity 1. Optional: Optional Lesson Instructions (Online)
This lesson is OPTIONAL. It is provided for students who seek enrichment or extra practice. You may skip this lesson.

If you choose to skip this lesson, then go to the Plan or Lesson Lists page and mark this lesson "Skipped" in order to proceed to the next lesson in the course.

Activity 2. Optional: Review Ancient Egyptian Gods (Online)

Activity 3. Optional: Lower Egypt and Upper Egypt (Online)

Activity 4. Optional: Lower Egypt and the Red Crown King (Online)

Activity 5. Optional: Upper Egypt and the White Crown King (Online)

Activity 6. Optional: King Narmer (Online)

Activity 7. Optional: The Narmer Palette (Online)

Activity 8. Optional: Lower Egypt and Upper Egypt (Online)

Activity 9. Optional: Show You Know (Online)

Activity 10. Optional: History Record Book (Online)

Activity 11. Optional: Egypt's Double Crown (Online)

Activity 12. Optional: The King's Portrait (Online)

Activity 13. Optional: The Egyptian Cinderella (Online)

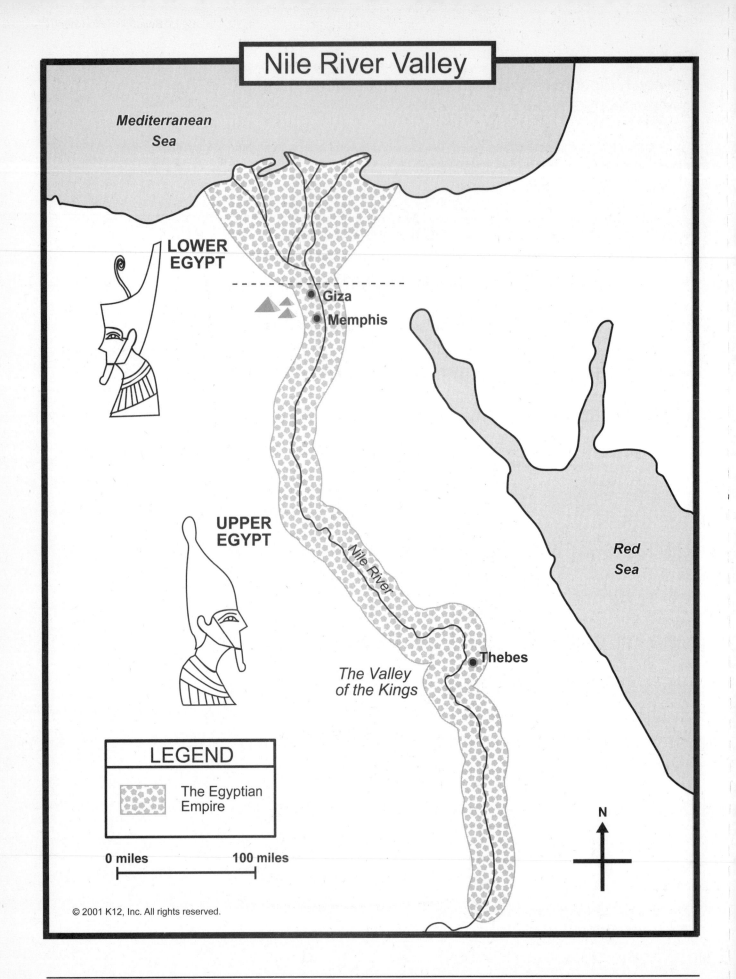

Nile River Valley

Mediterranean Sea

LOWER EGYPT

● Giza
● Memphis

UPPER EGYPT

Nile River

The Valley of the Kings

● Thebes

Red Sea

LEGEND

The Egyptian Empire

0 miles   100 miles

N

White Crown Cut-out Sheet

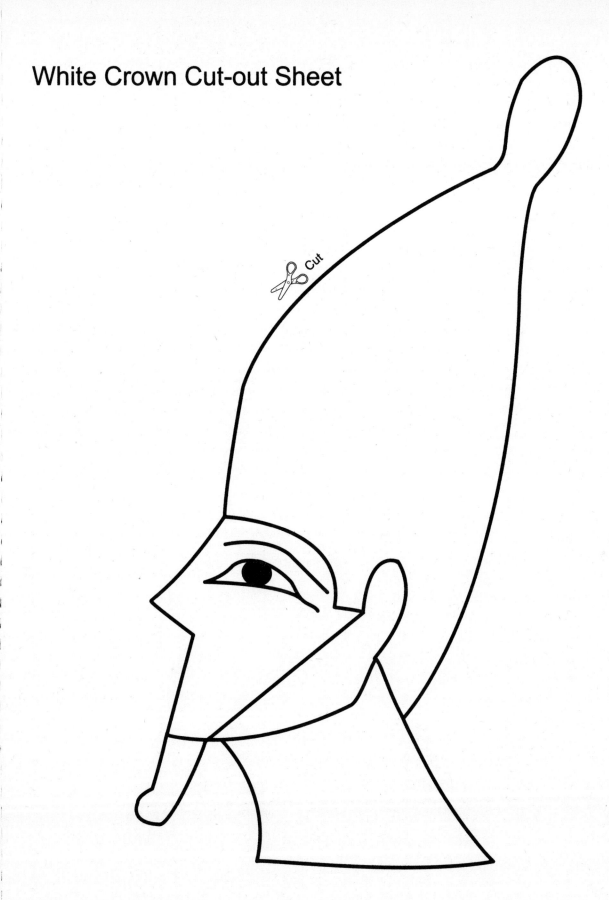

Red Crown Pattern Sheet

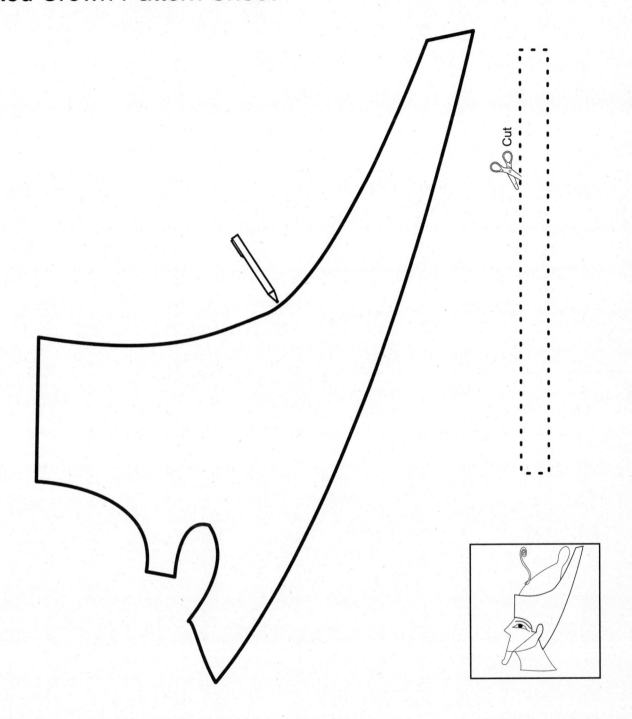

Student Guide
Lesson 7: Hieroglyphs

Lesson Objectives

- Explain that the ancient Egyptians wrote using hieroglyphs.
- Identify ways that writing helped civilization develop.

PREPARE

Approximate lesson time is 60 minutes.

Advance Preparation

- Please print an updated version of 'Hieroglyphs' and 'Papyrus' for today's lesson.

Materials

    For the Student

        crayons, 16 or more

        paper, 8 1/2" x 11"

        📖 Hieroglyphs

        📖 Papyrus

        Elmer's Glue-All

        paper, wax

        pencils, no. 2

        clay, colored

        brush, watercolor

        paints, watercolor, 8 colors or more

        The Winged Cat by Deborah Nourse Lattimore

Keywords and Pronunciation

cartouche (kahr-TOOSH)

hieroglyphs (HIY-ruh-glifs) : A way of picture writing in ancient Egypt that mixed picture symbols with letter-like characters.

LEARN
Activity 1: Writing Is Important (Online)

Activity 2: Writing in Ancient Egypt *(Online)*

Activity 3: Early Writing *(Online)*

Activity 4. Optional: Make Your Own Papyrus *(Online)*

Activity 5: Show You Know *(Online)*

Activity 6: History Record Book *(Online)*

Activity 7. Optional: Make a Cartouche *(Online)*

ASSESS
Lesson Assessment: Hieroglyphs (*Offline*)
You will complete an offline assessment covering the main objectives of this lesson. Your learning coach will score this assessment.

LEARN
Activity 8. Optional: Read About Hieroglyphs *(Online)*

Name _____   Date _____

Hieroglyphs

A vulture		**B** foot	
C	There is no C in ancient Eqyptian. Use "s" Use "k"	**Ch**	
D hand		**E** reed leaf	
F horned viper		**G** pot stand	
H shelter		**I** reed leaf	

Hieroglyphs

J — snake	K — basket with handle
L — lion	M — owl
N — water	O — lasso
P — foot stool	Q — hill
R — mouth	S — folded cloth

Hieroglyphs

T loaf of bread	**U** There is no U in ancient Eqyptian. Use "w"
V There is no V in ancient Eqyptian. Use "f"	**W** quail chick
X There is no X in ancient Eqyptian. Use "ks"	**Y** two reed leaves
Z doorbolt	

Name _____   Date _____

Papyrus

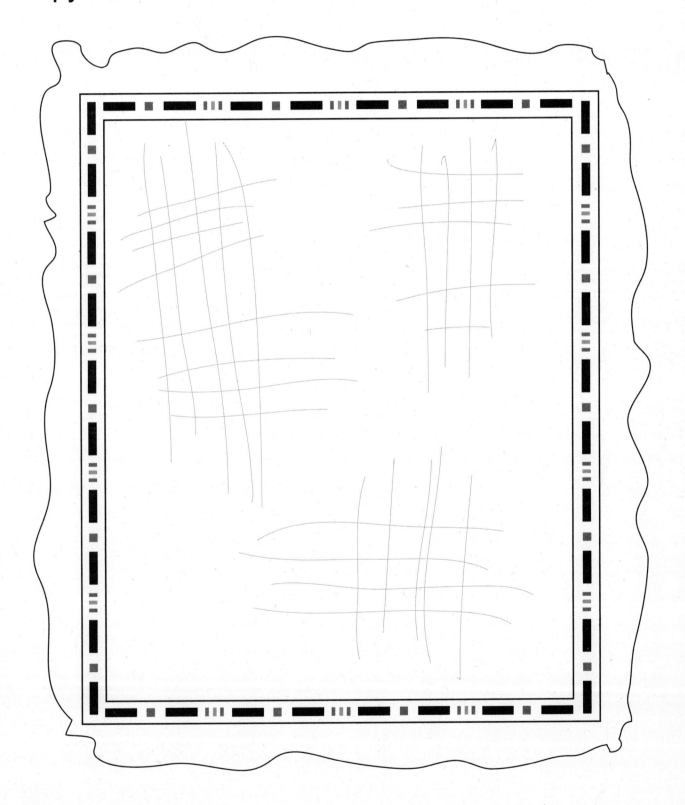

Name _____   Date _____

Lesson Assessment

Hieroglyphs

Short-Answer Questions:

1. What do we call the kind of writing the ancient Egyptians used?

2. What are some reasons why writing is so important?

Student Guide
Lesson 8. Optional: More Early Writing

Lesson Objectives

- Explain that the ancient Sumerians invented a kind of writing called cuneiform.
- Name two materials used for writing by the Egyptians and the Sumerians.

PREPARE

Approximate lesson time is 60 minutes.

Materials

For the Student

📖 Show You Know

pencils, no. 2

paper, 8 1/2" x 11"

pencils, colored, 16 or more

clay, colored

rolling pin

popsicle sticks

Growing Up In Ancient Egypt by Rosalie David

Keywords and Pronunciation

cuneiform (kyou-NEE-uh-form) : An ancient form of writing that uses wedge-shaped characters.

hieroglyphs (HIY-ruh-glifs) : A way of picture writing in ancient Egypt that mixed picture symbols with letter-like characters.

papyrus (puh-PIY-ruhs) : A plant used in ancient times to make a paper-like material for writing.

Sumer (SOO-mur)

Sumerians (soo-MEHR-ee-uhnz)

LEARN
Activity 1. Optional: Optional Lesson Instructions *(Online)*

This lesson is OPTIONAL. It is provided for students who seek enrichment or extra practice. You may skip this lesson.

If you choose to skip this lesson, then go to the Plan or Lesson Lists page and mark this lesson "Skipped" in order to proceed to the next lesson in the course.

Activity 2. Optional: The Egyptians and Their Writing (Online)

Activity 3. Optional: Picture Writing (Online)

Activity 4. Optional: Writing Made Easy (Online)

Activity 5. Optional: Show You Know (Online)

Activity 6. Optional: History Record Book (Online)

Activity 7. Optional: Creating Cuneiform (Online)

Activity 8. Optional: Reading and Talking (Offline)

Name _____   Date _____

Show You Know

Draw a line to match the word to the picture.

1. papyrus

2. hieroglyphs

3. cuneiform

Read the question and circle the word that fills in the blank.

4. Before the Egyptians started carving hieroglyphs, the _____ were writing cuneiform on clay tablets.

Sumerians   Mesopotamians   Egyptians

5. The _____ wrote on stone tablets until they learned to make paper out of papyrus.

Sumerians   Mesopotamians   Egyptians

Student Guide
Lesson 9: Mummies

Lesson Objectives

- Explain that mummies were buried with furniture, treasures, and food to keep them happy in the afterlife.
- Explain why the Egyptians wanted to preserve the bodies of the dead.

PREPARE

Approximate lesson time is 60 minutes.

Advance Preparation

- If you don't already have it, you will need the book *Mummies* by Joyce Milton for the activity in this lesson.

Materials

For the Student

    📖 map of the Nile River Valley

    Mummies by Joyce Milton (ISBN 0448413256)

    crayons, 16 or more

    pencils, no. 2

    paper, 8 1/2" x 11"

    📖 Amulet activity sheet

    pencils, colored, 16 or more

    Mummies Made in Egypt by Aliki

Keywords and Pronunciation

amulet : A symbol or sign that Egyptians believed would fight off evil spirits.

amulets (AM-yoo-lets)

ankh (ahngk)

archaeologist (ahr-kee-AH-luh-jist) : Someone who studies the buildings, tools, and other things left behind by people who lived in the past.

archaeologists (ahr-kee-AH-luh-jists)

mummy : A dead body that has been wrapped in cloth after being treated with special oils.

scarab (SKAIR-uhb) : A beetle that was a symbol of life after death in ancient Egypt.

LEARN
Activity 1: The Geography of Egypt *(Online)*

Activity 2: Why Mummies? *(Online)*

Activity 3: Archaeologists and Mummies *(Online)*

Activity 4: Show You Know *(Online)*

Activity 5: History Record Book *(Online)*

Activity 6. Optional: Egyptian Amulets *(Online)*

ASSESS
Lesson Assessment: Mummies (*Offline*)
You will complete an offline assessment covering the main objectives of this lesson. Your learning coach will score this assessment.

LEARN
Activity 7. Optional: Read About Mummies *(Online)*

Nile River Valley

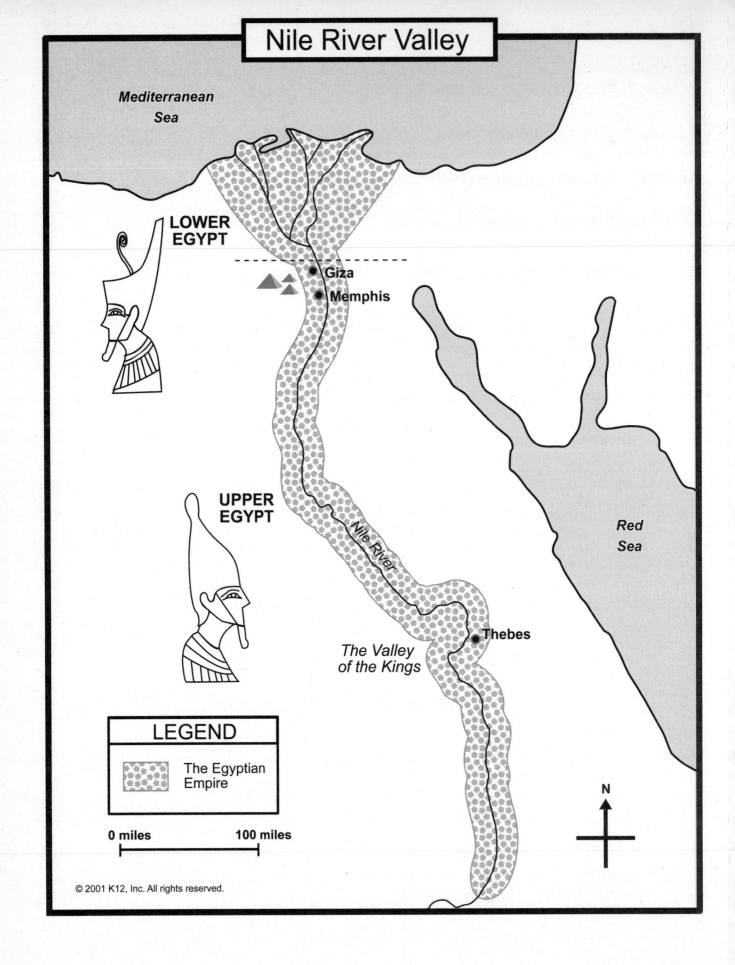

Mediterranean
Sea

LOWER
EGYPT

● Giza
● Memphis

UPPER
EGYPT

Nile River

Red
Sea

Thebes

The Valley
of the Kings

LEGEND

The Egyptian
Empire

0 miles   100 miles

N

88

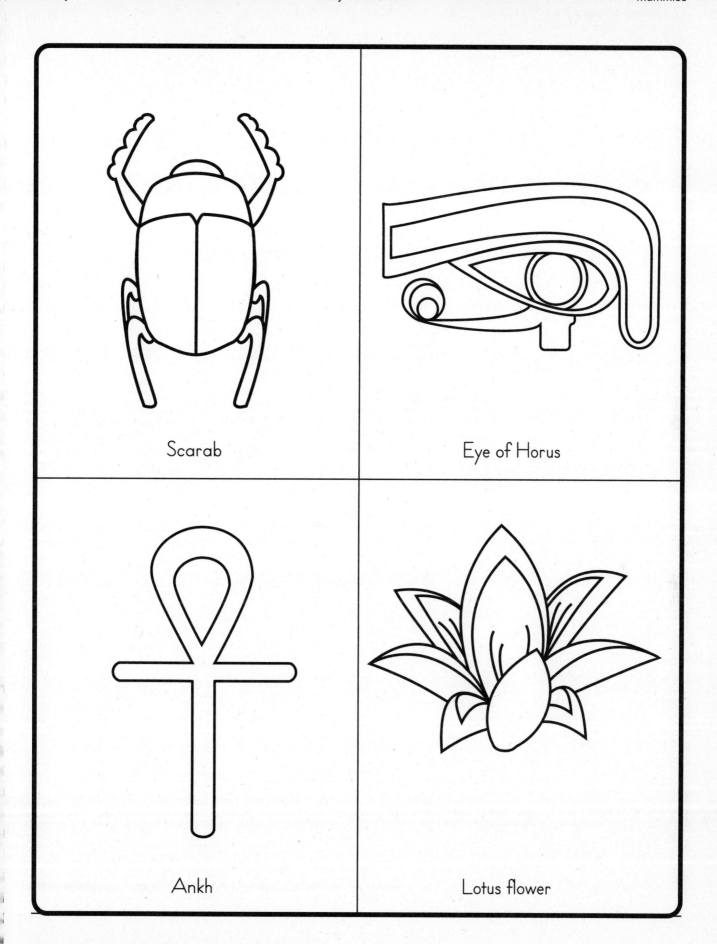

Scarab

Eye of Horus

Ankh

Lotus flower

Lesson Assessment

Mummies

Short-Answer Questions:

1. Why did the Egyptians think it was important to preserve dead bodies?

2. What did the Egyptians bury with their mummies?

Student Guide
Lesson 10: The Great Pyramid

Lesson Objectives

- Explain that the ancient Egyptians built pyramids for some pharaohs.
- Describe the ancient Egyptian pyramids as being built by hand.
- Identify the sphinx.

PREPARE

Approximate lesson time is 60 minutes.

Materials

For the Student

    🖼 map of the Nile River Valley

    🖼 Pyramid Construction

    scissors, round-end safety

    sugar cubes

    tape, clear

    🖼 The Amazing Maze

    pencils, no. 2

    🖼 Show You Know activity sheet

    paper, 8 1/2" x 11"

    pencils, colored, 16 or more

    cardboard, sheets

    crayons, 16 or more

    foil, aluminum

    glue sticks

    ruler, standard 12"

    markers, colored, 8 or more

    paper, colored construction, 12"x12"

    paper, tracing

    Pyramids of Ancient Egypt by John Clare

Keywords and Pronunciation

Giza (GEE-zuh)

Pharaoh Khufu (FAIR-oh KOO-foo)

pyramid : An ancient Egyptian stone building, which has a square base with outside walls of four triangles that meet in a point at the top.

sphinx (sfinks) : A large stone statue, found in the Egyptian desert, and having a lion's body with a person's head.

tomb : A place to bury a dead body.

LEARN
Activity 1: Why Mummies? *(Online)*

Activity 2: I Am the Great One *(Online)*

Activity 3: Eternal Homes *(Online)*

Activity 4: An Egyptian Watchdog *(Online)*

Activity 5: Show You Know *(Online)*

Activity 6: History Record Book *(Online)*

Activity 7. Optional: Build Your Own Pyramid *(Online)*

Activity 8. Optional: Making Your Own Maze *(Online)*

ASSESS
Lesson Assessment: The Great Pyramid (*Online*)
You will complete an offline assessment covering the main objectives of this lesson. Your learning coach will score this assessment.

LEARN
Activity 9. Optional: Reading About the Pyramids of Egypt *(Online)*

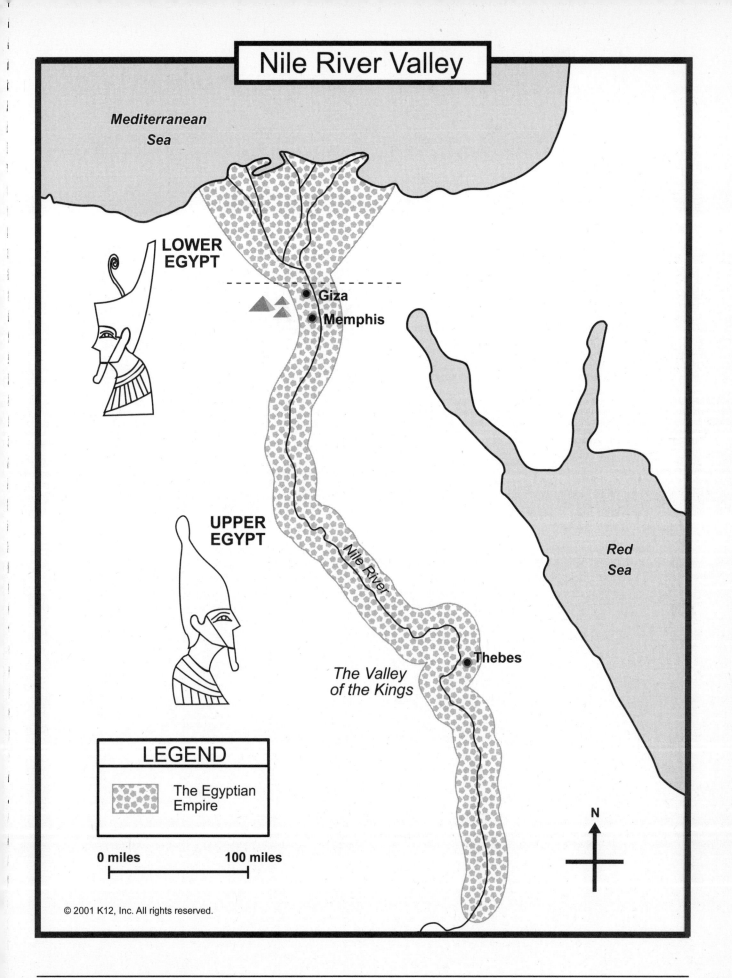

Nile River Valley

Mediterranean Sea

LOWER EGYPT

● **Giza**
● **Memphis**

UPPER EGYPT

Nile River

The Valley of the Kings

● **Thebes**

Red Sea

LEGEND

The Egyptian Empire

0 miles   100 miles

N

Make a Pyramid!

Decorate the inside of the pyramid, cut along the edges, then fold along the dotted lines. Tape up the four sides.

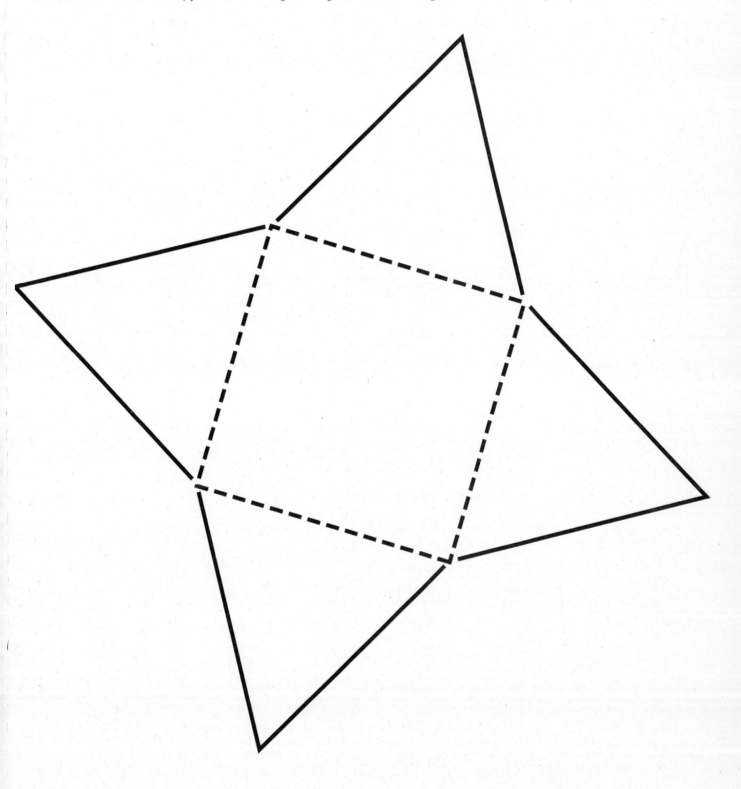

The Amazing Maze

Finish

Start

Name_____   Date_____

Show You Know

Circle the correct response to each question.

1. The Egyptians buried some of their pharaohs in giant stone
   tombs called_____.

   hieroglyphs   pyramids   cuneiforms

2. What were the pyramids made out of?

   steel   wood   stone

3. How did the Egyptians build pyramids?

   with big machines   by hand   with elephants

4. Which one of these pictures shows the Great Sphinx?

 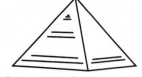 

Name _____   Date _____

Lesson Assessment

The Great Pyramid

Short Answer Questions:

1. The Egyptians buried their pharaohs in giant stone tombs called _____.

2. How did the Egyptians build the pyramids?

3. Which one of these pictures shows the Great Sphinx?

 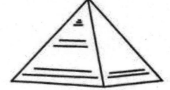 

Student Guide
Lesson 11: Tutankhamen - King Tut

Lesson Objectives

- Identify King Tut as an Egyptian pharaoh.
- Explain that, unlike most other tombs, Tutankhamen's tomb had not been robbed.
- Name two of the artifacts found in King Tut's tomb.

PREPARE

Approximate lesson time is 60 minutes.

Advance Preparation

- If you don't already have it, you will need the book Tut's Mummy: Lost...and Found by Judy Donnelly for the activity in this lesson.
- If you don't already have it, you will need *Tutankhamen's Gift* by Robert Sabuda for the optional activity in this lesson.

Materials

For the Student

- map of the Nile River Valley
- Discussion Guide activity sheet

  Tut's Mummy: Lost...and Found by Judy Donnelly (ISBN 0394891899)

  pencils, no. 2

  paper, 8 1/2" x 11"

  pencils, colored, 16 or more

- King Tut's Death Mask

  crayons, 16 or more

  globe, inflatable

  markers, colored, 8 or more

  yarn

  paper, drawing, 12" x 18"

  Tutankhamen's Gift by Robert Sabuda

Keywords and Pronunciation

Tutankhamen (too-tahng-KAH-muhn)

LEARN
Activity 1: The Egyptian Pharaohs (Online)

Activity 2: Keeping It a Secret (Online)

Activity 3: Getting to Know King Tutankhamen (Online)

Activity 4: Show You Know (Online)

Activity 5: History Record Book (Online)

Activity 6. Optional: Color Tut's Mask (Online)

Activity 7. Optional: Two Types of Tombs (Online)

ASSESS
Lesson Assessment: Tutankhamen – King Tut (*Offline*)
You will complete an offline assessment covering the main objectives of this lesson. Your learning coach will score this assessment.

LEARN
Activity 8. Optional: Read *Tutankhamen's Gift* (Online)

Nile River Valley

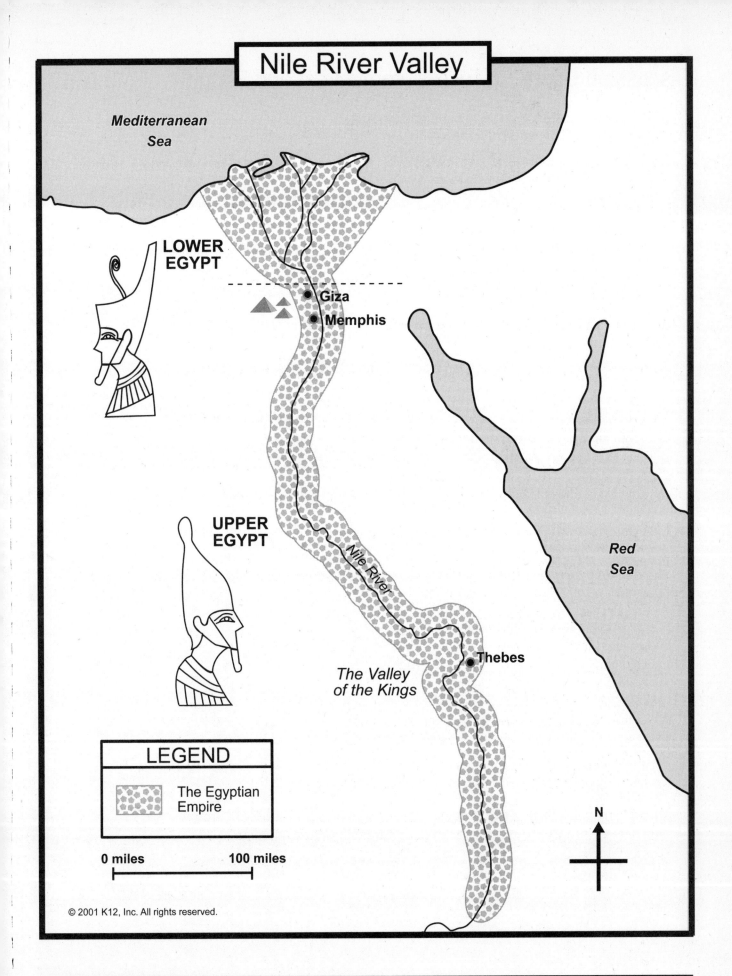

Mediterranean
Sea

LOWER
EGYPT

Giza

Memphis

UPPER
EGYPT

Nile River

Red
Sea

Thebes

The Valley
of the Kings

LEGEND

The Egyptian
Empire

0 miles   100 miles

N

Discussion Guide for Tut's Mummy: Lost and Found

Before reading pages 4 and 5 ask the questions:
What do you see in the picture? What do you think is wrong with the man who is lying down?

Egyptians, men and women, a woman with an unusual-looking hat, a man wearing a leopard skin, and a man lying down who looks sick or dead.

After reading page 8, ask the questions:
What do you see in the picture? Point out the jars to hold the pharaoh's internal organs.

The Egyptians are turning the body into a mummy.

After reading pages 10 and 11, ask the question:
Can you find the queen in the picture?

She is in the background on the left side of page 10. She is wearing a crown.

After reading page 12, turn back to pages 10 and 11, then ask the question:
Can you find the priest who is dressed as Anubis in this picture?

He is in the middle of the picture, in the front. His black mask looks like a dog's head, but it is really the head of a doglike animal called a jackal.

After reading through page 17, ask the question:
Were the Egyptians happy or sad about Tutankhamen's death?

Sad because he died, but happy because they believed he was going to a new life.

After reading page 24, ask the question:
Who was Tutankhamen?

He was a pharaoh—or king—of Egypt long, long ago.

While reading pages 34 and 35, ask the questions:
What do you see? What do you think the Egyptians did with some of these things?

Accept any reasonable responses.

After finishing the book, ask the question:
Why did Howard Carter send Tutankhamen's treasures to a museum?

Because he wanted many people to be able to see and enjoy the treasures.

King Tutankhamen

Lesson Assessment

Tutankhamen – King Tut

Short-Answer Questions:

1. Who was Tutankhamen?

2. Why is tutankhamen's tomb considered so special?

3. What types of treasures were buried in King Tut's tomb?

Student Guide
Lesson 12: The Egyptian Cinderella

Lesson Objectives

- Demonstrate mastery of important knowledge and skills taught in this unit.
- Identify the Fertile Crescent as an area where nomads settled.
- Explain that in Mesopotamia and other regions farmers needed to irrigate, or transport, water to help their crops grow.
- Recall that regular flooding of the Nile leaves behind good soil for farming.
- Find the Nile River on a map.
- Know that the ancient Egyptians worshipped many gods.
- Explain that the ancient Egyptians wrote using hieroglyphs.
- Explain why the Egyptians wanted to preserve the bodies of the dead.
- Explain that the ancient Egyptians built pyramids for some pharaohs.

PREPARE

Approximate lesson time is 60 minutes.

Materials

For the Student

- map of the Nile River Valley
- map, world
- History Record Book
- Egyptian Cinderella Discussion Questions
- The Egyptian Cinderella by Shirley Climo (ISBN 0064432793)
- A Princess's Slipper
- crayons, 16 or more
- Elmer's Glue-All
- glitter
- markers, colored, 8 or more

Keywords and Pronunciation

Rhodopis (rah-DOH-pes)

LEARN
Activity 1: Review of the Nile River Valley *(Online)*

Activity 2: Reviewing Unit Two (Online)

ASSESS
Unit Assessment: Early Civilizations (Offline)

Complete an offline Unit Assessment. Your learning coach will score this part of the Assessment.

LEARN
Activity 3. Optional: The Egyptian Cinderella (Online)

Activity 4. Optional: A Princess's Slipper (Online)

Activity 2: Reviewing Unit Two (Online)

Nile River Valley

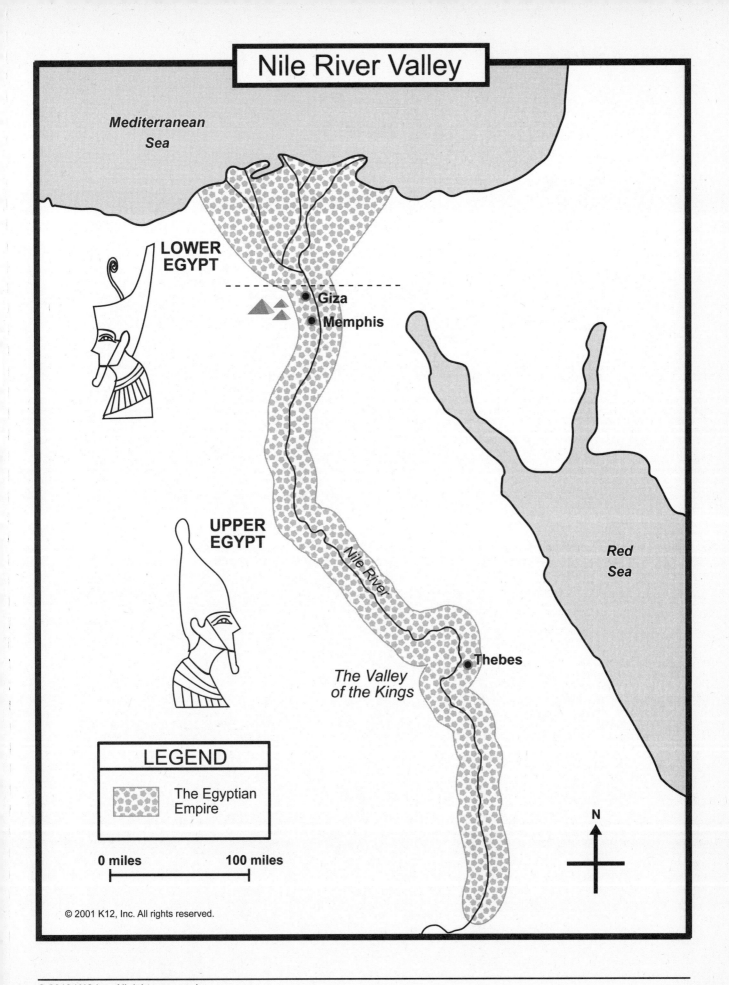

Mediterranean Sea

LOWER EGYPT

● Giza
● Memphis

UPPER EGYPT

Nile River

Red Sea

The Valley of the Kings

● Thebes

LEGEND

The Egyptian Empire

0 miles   100 miles

N

113

Name _____   Date _____

Early Civilizations

For questions 1 - 9, read each question out loud. Then read each answer. Fill in the bubble next to the correct answer. For question 10, complete the map activity.

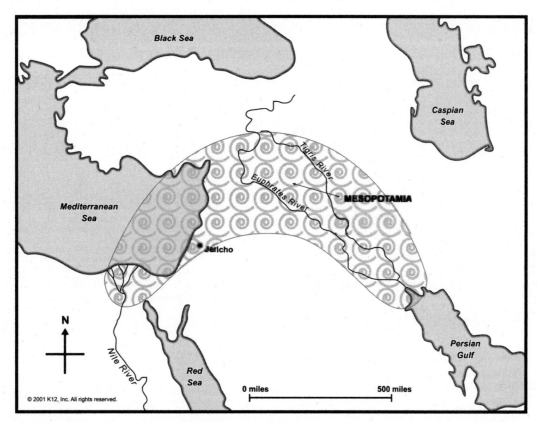

1. Mesopotamian nomads settled in the area shown on the map. What is this area called?
    ○ the desert
    ○ the Fertile Crescent
    ○ the Nile River Valley

2. Did ancient Egyptians and Mesopotamians worship one god or many gods?
    ○ one
    ○ many

3. Who built the pyramids?
   - ○ Mesopotamians
   - ○ Egyptians
   - ○ Nomads

4. Why did the ancient Egyptians preserve the bodies of the dead?
   - ○ So they could display them in museums where millions of people could see them.
   - ○ They believed people went on to live in another world and would need their bodies.
   - ○ They wanted their family members to be able to recognize them always.

5. What is ancient Egyptian writing called?
   - ○ hieroglyphs
   - ○ cuneiform
   - ○ cursive

6. What did the Nile River do every year?
   - ○ It dried up.
   - ○ It froze into solid ice.
   - ○ It flooded and left behind rich soil.

7. What was the ruler of ancient Egypt called?
   - ○ pharaoh
   - ○ king
   - ○ prince

8. The civilizations of ancient Egypt and Mesopotamia began near

   _____.

   ○ rivers

   ○ roads

   ○ mountains

9. What does *Mesopotamia* mean?

   ○ between the mountains

   ○ between the rivers

   ○ between the villages

10. Draw a circle around the Nile River on the map below.

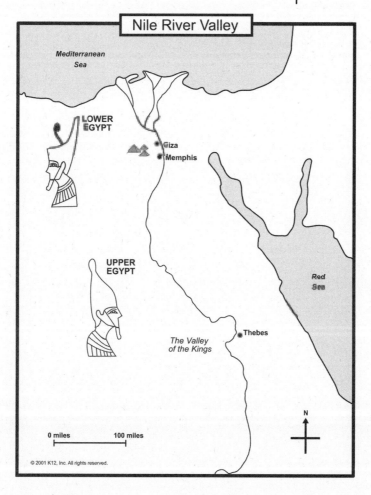

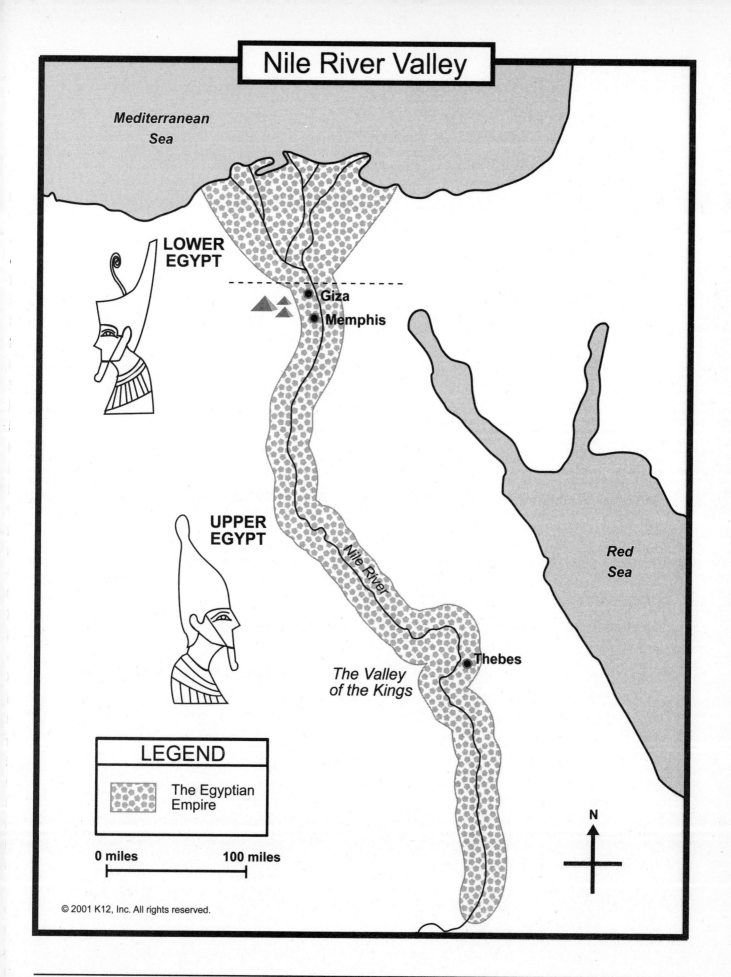

Nile River Valley

Mediterranean
Sea

LOWER EGYPT

Giza

Memphis

UPPER EGYPT

Nile River

Thebes

*The Valley
of the Kings*

*Red
Sea*

LEGEND

The Egyptian
Empire

0 miles   100 miles

N

Egyptian Cinderella Discussion Questions

After reading page 1, have the child look at the picture, then ask the question:
Which girl do you think is Rhodopis (rah-DOH-pes)?

Rhodopis is the one blushing.

After reading page 2, ask the question:
Why is Rhodopis blushing?

The Egyptian girls are teasing her.

After reading the first paragraph on page 6, have the child:
Find the monkey and the hippopotamus on the page.

After reading the first two paragraphs on page 8, ask the questions:
How do you think the servant girls feel about Rhodopis's new slippers?
Does Rhodopis look happy? How can you tell?

They're jealous. No. Rhodopis is crying, frowning, and sitting by herself.

As you read page 9, have the child:
Find the girl wearing the necklace of blue beads, the girl wearing the bracelets, and the girl wearing the many-colored sash.

Before reading page 15, have the child look at the pictures, then ask the questions:
What do you see? Who is the man on the right side of the page? Do you remember what his crown is called?

The pharaoh. The Double Crown; the Red Crown and the White Crown of a united Egypt.

After reading page 25, have the child find Rhodopis in the rushes, then ask the question:
What are rushes?

Rushes are long grasses by the water.

The Egyptian Cinderella's Slipper

Student Guide
Lesson 1: Pyramids and Ziggurats

Explore the highly developed civilizations of Egypt and Mesopotamia, which grew with strong leaders, formal religions, and great monuments, such as pyramids and ziggurats. Ancient Judaism emerged against this background. In addition the first set of written laws, called the Code of Hammurabi, offered rules to rich and poor alike.

Lesson Objectives

- Explain that monuments such as pyramids and ziggurats were built to honor the gods worshipped by people in ancient civilizations.
- Identify Mesopotamian temples as ziggurats.
- Identify a picture of a ziggurat.

PREPARE

Approximate lesson time is 60 minutes.

Materials

For the Student

    🖳 map of Mesopotamia

    crayons, 16 or more - orange

    pencils, no. 2

    paper, 8 1/2" x 11"

    pencils, colored, 16 or more

    cookie sheet

    watering can

    clay, colored - self-hardening brown

Keywords and Pronunciation

ziggurat (ZIH-guh-rat) : A temple tower of the ancient Mesopotamians that looks like a pyramid with stepped sides.

LEARN
Activity 1: Buried in Style *(Online)*

Activity 2: Mighty Monuments *(Online)*

Activity 3: Temples to the Gods *(Online)*

Activity 4: Show You Know *(Online)*

Activity 5: History Record Book *(Online)*

Activity 6. Optional: From Ziggurats to Mounds of Dirt *(Online)*

Activity 7. Optional: Make a Ziggurat *(Online)*

ASSESS

Lesson Assessment: Pyramids and Ziggurats (*Online*)

You will complete an offline assessment covering the main objectives of this lesson. Your learning coach will score this assessment.

LEARN

Activity 8. Optional: Mesopotamian Gods and Goddesses *(Online)*

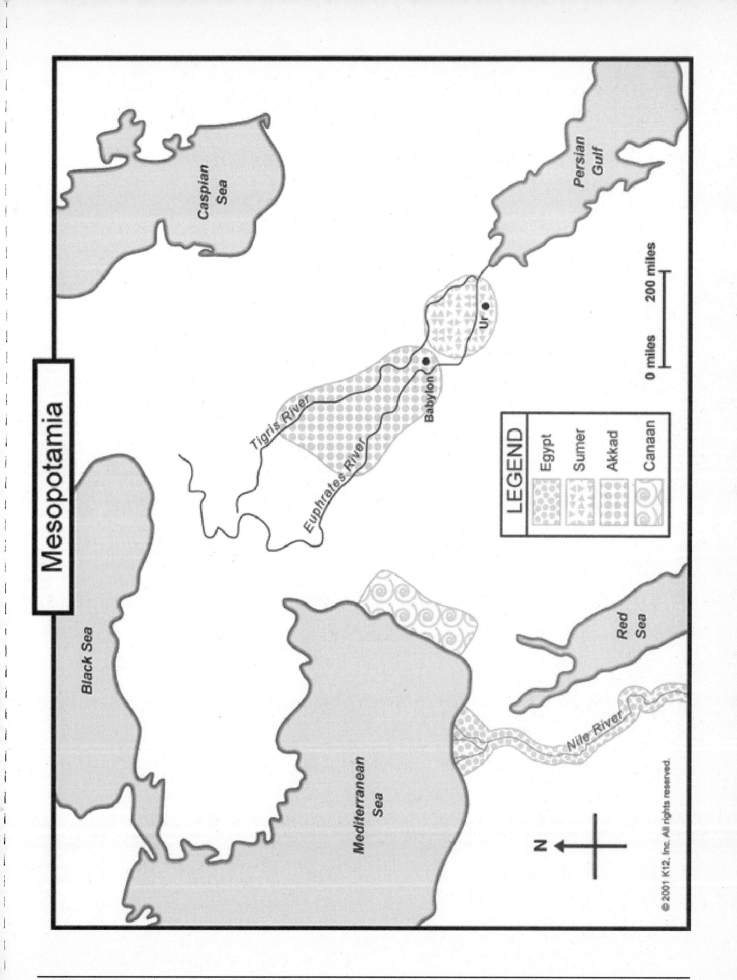

Mesopotamia

Caspian Sea

Persian Gulf

Black Sea

Tigris River

Euphrates River

Babylon

Ur

0 miles

200 miles

LEGEND

Egypt

Sumer

Akkad

Canaan

Mediterranean Sea

Red Sea

Nile River

N

© 2001 K12, Inc. All rights reserved.

125

Name _____   Date _____

Lesson Assessment

Pyramids and Ziggurats

Short-Answer Questions:

1. What were Mesopotamian temples called?

2. Why did the people in ancient Mesopotamia build ziggurats?

3. Which of the following pictures shows a ziggurat?

Student Guide
Lesson 2. Optional: Sargon Conquers Mesopotamia

Lesson Objectives

- Identify Sargon as a ruler who united Mesopotamia.
- Define military dictatorship.
- Locate Mesopotamia, the Tigris River, and the Euphrates River on a map.

PREPARE

Approximate lesson time is 60 minutes.

Materials

For the Student

    🖳 map of Mesopotamia

    crayons, 16 or more - yellow, pink

    crayons, 16 or more

    pencils, no. 2

    paper, 8 1/2" x 11"

    paper, drawing, 12" x 18"

    pencils, colored, 16 or more

    🖳 Sargon Unites Mesopotamia activity sheet

    Ancient Egyptians and Their Neighbors: An Activity Guide by Marian Broida

Keywords and Pronunciation

Akkad (AK-ad)

military dictatorship : A government that uses military power, or soldiers, to enforce the law.

Sargon (SAHR-gahn)

Sumer (SOO-mur)

Sumerians (soo-MEHR-ee-uhnz)

LEARN
Activity 1. Optional: Optional Lesson Instructions *(Online)*

This lesson is OPTIONAL. It is provided for students who seek enrichment or extra practice. You may skip this lesson.

If you choose to skip this lesson, then go to the Plan or Lesson Lists page and mark this lesson "Skipped" in order to proceed to the next lesson in the course.

Activity 2. Optional: Map of Mesopotamia *(Online)*

Activity 3. Optional: The History of Sargon *(Online)*

Activity 4. Optional: Show You Know *(Online)*

Activity 5. Optional: History Record Book *(Online)*

Activity 6. Optional: What Did Sargon Do? *(Online)*

Activity 7. Optional: Sargon Unites Mesopotamia *(Online)*

Activity 8. Optional: Read About Sumerian Culture *(Online)*

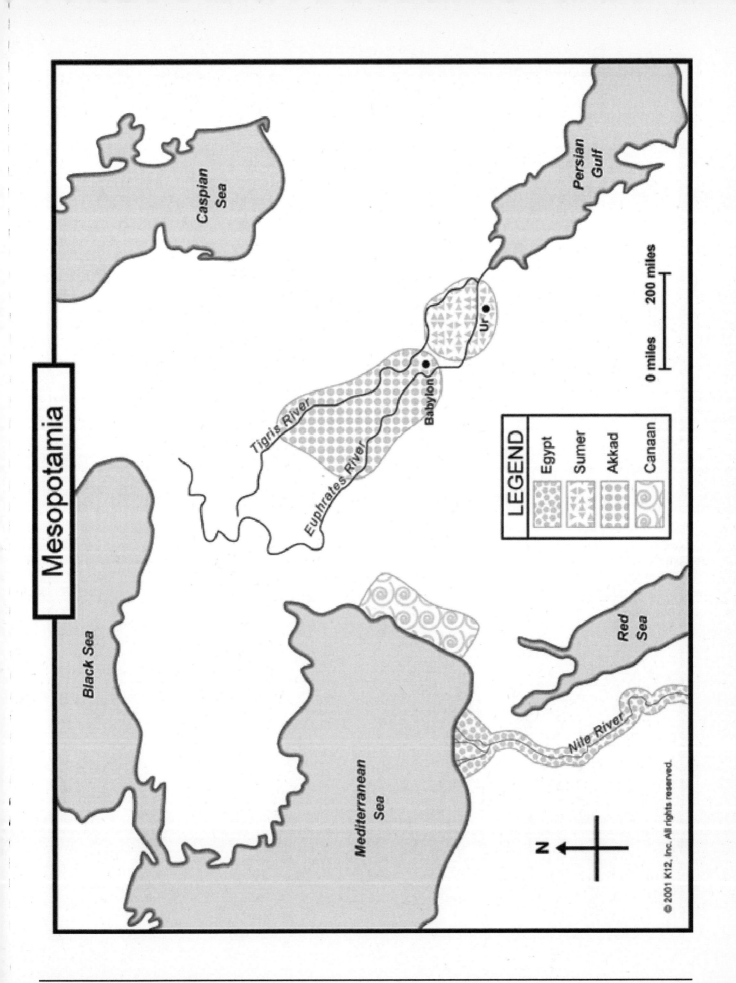

Mesopotamia

Caspian Sea

Persian Gulf

Tigris River

Euphrates River

Babylon

Ur

Black Sea

Mediterranean Sea

Red Sea

Nile River

LEGEND

Egypt

Sumer

Akkad

Canaan

0 miles

200 miles

N

© 2001 K12, Inc. All rights reserved.

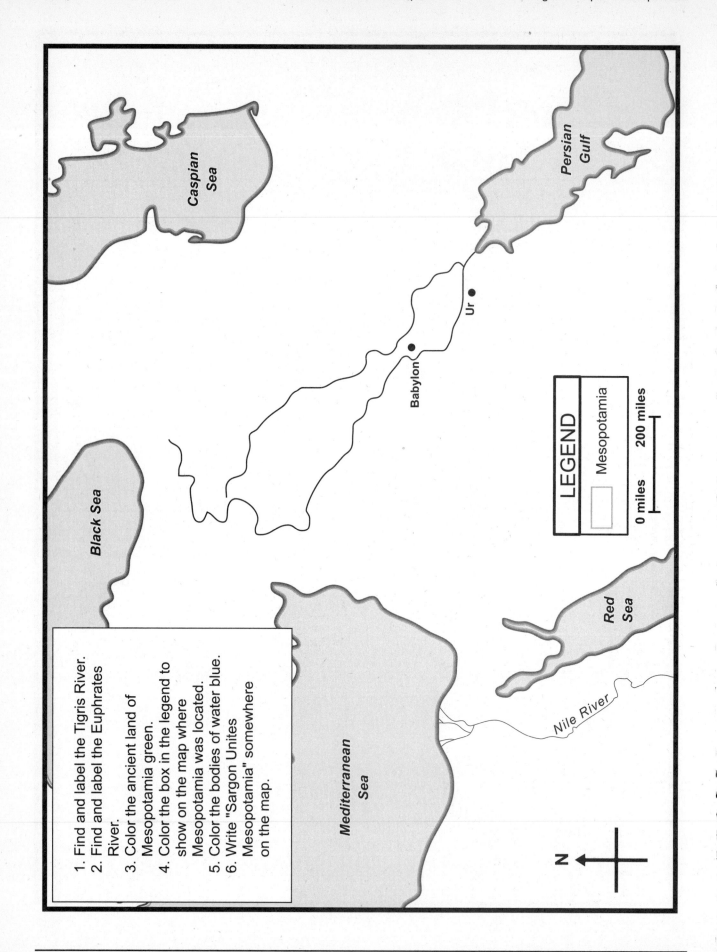

Caspian Sea

Persian Gulf

Ur

Babylon

Black Sea

LEGEND

Mesopotamia

0 miles   200 miles

Red Sea

Mediterranean Sea

Nile River

1. Find and label the Tigris River.
2. Find and label the Euphrates River.
3. Color the ancient land of Mesopotamia green.
4. Color the box in the legend to show on the map where Mesopotamia was located.
5. Color the bodies of water blue.
6. Write "Sargon Unites Mesopotamia" somewhere on the map.

N

Student Guide
Lesson 3: Abraham Goes to Canaan

The ancient Egyptians and Mesopotamians believed in many gods. But thousands of years ago in Mesopotamia, a new religion began. This religion is called Judaism. It teaches the worship of one God. Much of what we know about the story of Abraham, and the beginnings of Judaism, is told in the Hebrew Bible.

Lesson Objectives

- Identify Judaism as the religion of Abraham.
- Explain why Abraham went to Canaan.
- Know that the followers of Judaism believe in one God.

PREPARE

Approximate lesson time is 60 minutes.

Materials

For the Student

    🖳 map of Mesopotamia

    pencils, no. 2

    paper, 8 1/2" x 11"

    pencils, colored, 16 or more

    markers, colored, 8 or more

    🖳 Abraham's Language activity sheet

Keywords and Pronunciation

Canaan (KAY-nuhn)

ziggurat (ZIH-guh-rat) : A temple tower of the ancient Mesopotamians that looks like a pyramid with stepped sides.

LEARN
Activity 1: Mesopotamia Review (Online)

Activity 2: Abraham and Judaism (Online)

Activity 3: Show You Know (Online)

Activity 4: History Record Book *(Online)*

Activity 5. Optional: Retrace Abraham's Travels *(Online)*

Activity 6. Optional: Abraham's Language *(Online)*

ASSESS

Lesson Assessment: Abraham Goes to Canaan (*Offline*)

You will complete an offline assessment covering the main objectives of this lesson. Your learning coach will score this assessment.

LEARN

Activity 7. Optional: Canaan *(Online)*

Mesopotamia

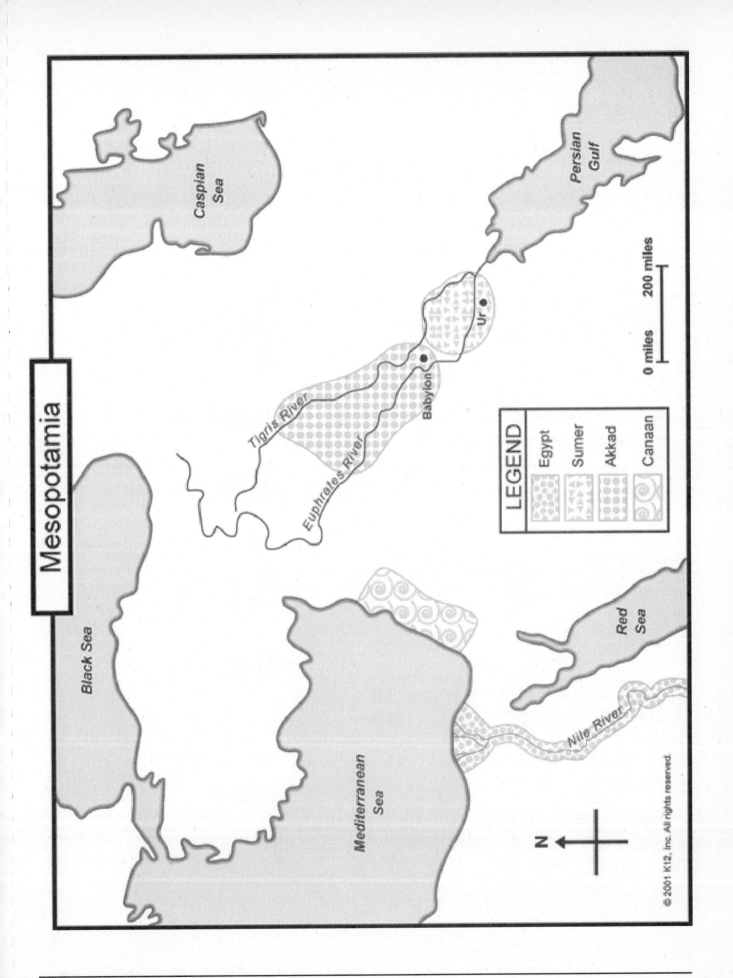

LEGEND

Egypt
Sumer
Akkad
Canaan

Caspian Sea

Persian Gulf

Tigris River

Euphrates River

Babylon

Ur

0 miles   200 miles

Black Sea

Mediterranean Sea

Red Sea

Nile River

N

© 2001 K12, Inc. All rights reserved.

Name _____   Date _____

Abraham's Language

Hebrew is the language of the Hebrew Bible and the State of Israel, which is where Canaan was located in the time of Abraham. Learn to write some of this language by tracing over the Hebrew letters. Then try writing some yourself.

English	Hebrew	Your Turn

Represents the number 1.
Can mean bull, strength, or leader.

א

Represents the number 2.
Can mean tent, house, or household.

ב

Represents the number 3.
Can mean camel, pride. or to lift up.

ג

Represents the number 4.
Can mean door, pathway, or to enter.

ד

Represents the number 5.
Can mean window, fence, or to reveal.

ה

Name _____   Date _____

Lesson Assessment

Abraham Goes to Canaan

Short-Answer Questions:

1. Why did Abraham and his family move to a new land?

2. What is the name of the religion of Abraham?

3. Do the Jewish people believe in one God or many gods and goddesses?

Student Guide
Lesson 4: Joseph and the Coat of Many Colors

Thousands of years ago in Mesopotamia a new religion began, called Judaism. This religion taught the worship of just one God. Much of what we know about the beginnings of Judaism comes from old writings, including the book called the Hebrew Bible. Today you'll hear a story from this book about Joseph and his coat of many colors.

Lesson Objectives

- Identify Abraham's many descendants as the Israelites, or the Jewish people.

PREPARE

Approximate lesson time is 60 minutes.

Materials

For the Student

    📖 map of Mesopotamia

    pencils, no. 2

    paper, 8 1/2" x 11"

    pencils, colored, 16 or more

    crayons, 16 or more

    paper, colored construction, 12"x12"

    markers, colored, 8 or more

    paints, watercolor, 8 colors or more

    penny

Keywords and Pronunciation

biblical : Relating to the Bible.

Israelite : A member of the Jewish people.

Potiphar (PAHT-uh-fur)

LEARN
Activity 1: History Questions *(Online)*

Activity 2: The Story of Joseph *(Online)*

Activity 3: Show You Know *(Online)*

Activity 4: History Record Book *(Online)*

Activity 5. Optional: Draw Joseph's Coat *(Online)*

Activity 6. Optional: Create a Family Tree *(Online)*

ASSESS

Lesson Assessment: Joseph and the Coat of Many Colors (*Offline*)

You will complete an offline assessment covering the main objectives of this lesson. Your learning coach will score this assessment.

LEARN

Activity 7. Optional: Hear Joseph's Story in Song *(Online)*

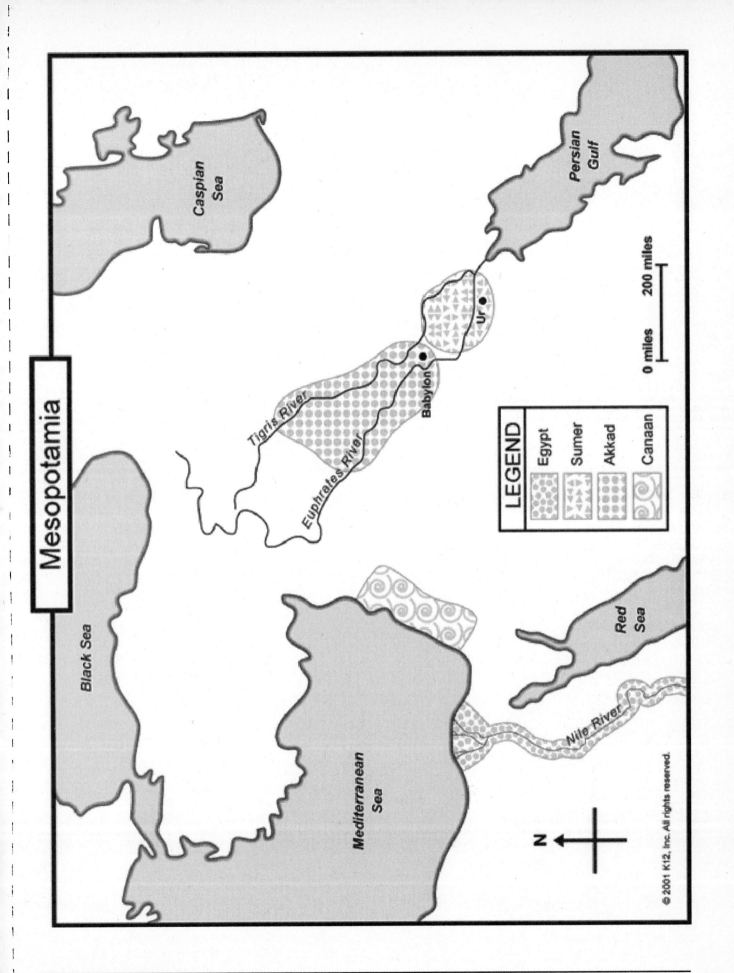

Mesopotamia

Black Sea

Caspian
Sea

Persian
Gulf

Tigris River

Euphrates River

Babylon

Ur

200 miles

0 miles

LEGEND

Egypt

Sumer

Akkad

Canaan

Mediterranean
Sea

Red
Sea

Nile River

N

© 2001 K12, Inc. All rights reserved.

Lesson Assessment

Joseph and the Coat of Many Colors

Short-Answer Question:

1. What is the name of the people who are descended from Abraham?

Student Guide
Lesson 5: The Israelites Go to Egypt

Lesson Objectives

- Know that the Israelites left Canaan and went to Egypt.
- Know that the Jewish people worshipped only one God.
- Know that Joseph interpreted the pharaoh's dreams.

PREPARE

Approximate lesson time is 60 minutes.

Materials

For the Student

    🖥 map of Mesopotamia

    crayons, 16 or more

    pencils, no. 2

    paper, 8 1/2" x 11"

    markers, colored, 8 or more

    pencils, colored, 16 or more

    🖥 Picture Timeline activity sheet

    glue sticks

    paper, colored construction, 12"x12"

    scissors, round-end safety

    Joseph by Brian Wildsmith

Keywords and Pronunciation

famine : A shortage of food.

worship : A way to thank God through prayer.

LEARN
Activity 1: Question and Answer (Online)

Activity 2: Joseph's Dream (Online)

Activity 3: Show You Know *(Online)*

Activity 4: History Record Book *(Online)*

Activity 5. Optional: Pharaoh's Dream *(Online)*

Activity 6. Optional: Picture Timeline *(Online)*

ASSESS

Lesson Assessment: The Israelites Go to Egypt *(Offline)*

You will complete an offline assessment covering the main objectives of this lesson. Your learning coach will score this assessment.

LEARN
Activity 7. Optional: Joseph *(Online)*

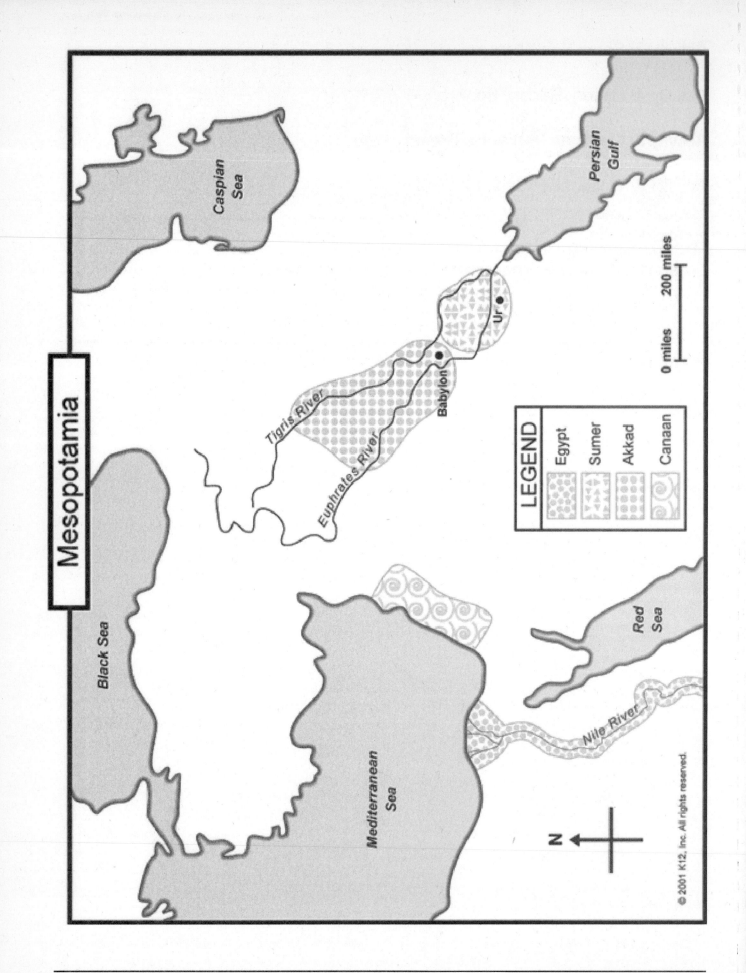

Mesopotamia

LEGEND

Egypt
Sumer
Akkad
Canaan

Caspian Sea

Persian Gulf

Tigris River

Euphrates River

Babylon

Ur

Black Sea

Mediterranean Sea

Red Sea

Nile River

0 miles 200 miles

N

© 2001 K12, Inc. All rights reserved.

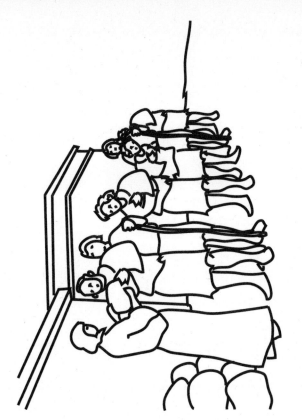

During the time of famine, Joseph hands out grain to the hungry.

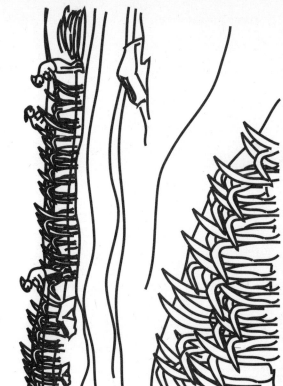

For seven years the Nile flooded and the crops grew well.

 cut

Joseph explains a prisoner's dream.

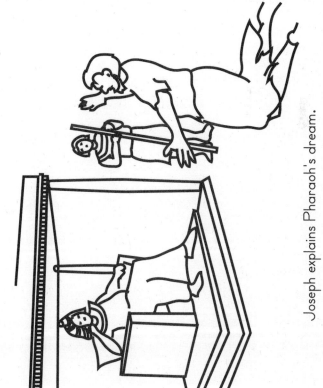

Joseph explains Pharaoh's dream.

Lesson Assessment

The Israelites Go to Egypt

Short-Answer Questions:

1. Who interpreted Pharaoh's dream?

2. How many gods did the Jewish people worship?

3. Where were the Israelites living before they went to Egypt?

Student Guide
Lesson 6: The Tower of Babel

Lesson Objectives

- Identify Babylon as a large, powerful city in Mesopotamia.
- Identify ziggurat as the name for the temple the Babylonians built to worship their gods.
- Know that the story from the Hebrew Bible about the Tower of Babel is about why there are different languages.

PREPARE

Approximate lesson time is 60 minutes.

Materials

For the Student

🖥 map of Babylon and Assyria

crayons, 16 or more

pencils, no. 2

paper, 8 1/2" x 11"

twig

bowl

household items - dirt, straw or hay

newspaper - or magazines

shoeboxes

water

camera

Legos

blocks

Pieter Bruegel's Tower of Babel: The Builder With the Red Hat by Nils Jockel

Keywords and Pronunciation

Babel (BA-buhl)

Babylon (BA-buh-lahn)

LEARN
Activity 1: Return to Mesopotamia *(Online)*

Activity 2: The Busy City of Babylon *(Online)*

Activity 3: The Tower of Babel *(Online)*

Activity 4: The Remains of Babylon *(Online)*

Activity 5: Show You Know *(Online)*

Activity 6: History Record Book *(Online)*

Activity 7. Optional: Make a Mesopotamian Brick *(Online)*

Activity 8. Optional: Lego Babylon *(Online)*

ASSESS

Lesson Assessment: The Tower of Babel (*Offline*)

You will complete an offline assessment covering the main objectives of this lesson. Your learning coach will score this assessment.

LEARN
Activity 9. Optional: The Builder With the Red Hat *(Online)*

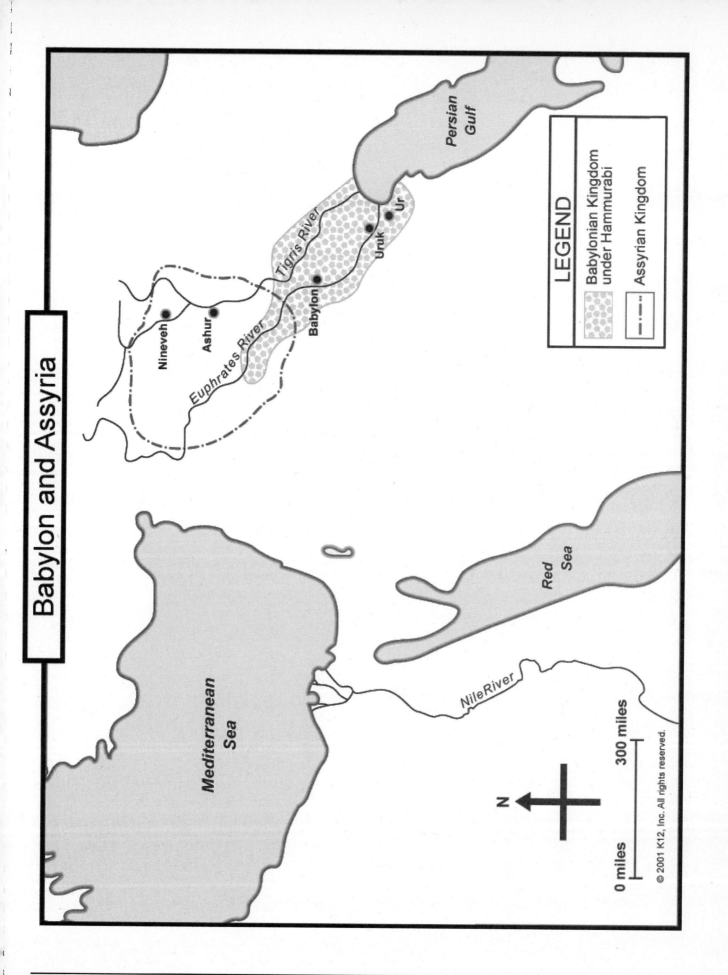

Babylon and Assyria

LEGEND

Babylonian Kingdom under Hammurabi

Assyrian Kingdom

Persian Gulf

Tigris River

Euphrates River

Nineveh

Ashur

Babylon

Uruk

Ur

Mediterranean Sea

Red Sea

Nile River

N

0 miles

300 miles

© 2001 K12, Inc. All rights reserved.

Name _____   Date _____

Lesson Assessment

The Tower of Babel

Short-Answer Questions:

1. Was Babylon a big, powerful city or a small village?

2. Where was Babylon located?

3. What did the Babylonians call the temples they built to worship their gods?

4. In the Bible story, what did God do to stop the proud people from building the Tower of Babel?

Student Guide
Lesson 7: Hammurabi, The Fair King

Many rulers of the ancient world used military force to keep order. But Hammurabi, king of Babylon, also used laws to keep order. The Code of Hammurabi was the first written set of laws. Although the laws might seem harsh to us today, they tried to be fair to both rich and poor.

Lesson Objectives
- Identify reasons why laws are important to civilization.
- Identify the Code of Hammurabi as the first written set of laws.

PREPARE

Approximate lesson time is 60 minutes.

Materials
.For the Student
- 🖥 map of Babylon and Assyria
- crayons, 16 or more
- pencils, no. 2
- paper, 8 1/2" x 11"
- markers, colored, 8 or more
- The Ancient Near East: A Bellerophon Coloring Book

Keywords and Pronunciation
Hammurabi (ha-muh-RAH-bee)

justice : Treating everyone fairly.

oppress : Treating people unfairly by not letting them improve their lives.

tyrant : An unfair ruler who treats people cruelly.

LEARN
Activity 1: Why Are Laws Important? (Online)

Activity 2: Hammurabi, The Fair King (Online)

Activity 3: A Code of Laws *(Online)*

Activity 4: Show You Know *(Online)*

Activity 5: History Record Book *(Online)*

Activity 6. Optional: Draw the Law *(Online)*

Activity 7. Optional: Write a Law *(Online)*

ASSESS

Lesson Assessment: Hammurabi, The Fair King *(Offline)*

You will complete an offline assessment covering the main objectives of this lesson. Your learning coach will score this assessment.

LEARN

Activity 8. Optional: Color Pictures *(Online)*

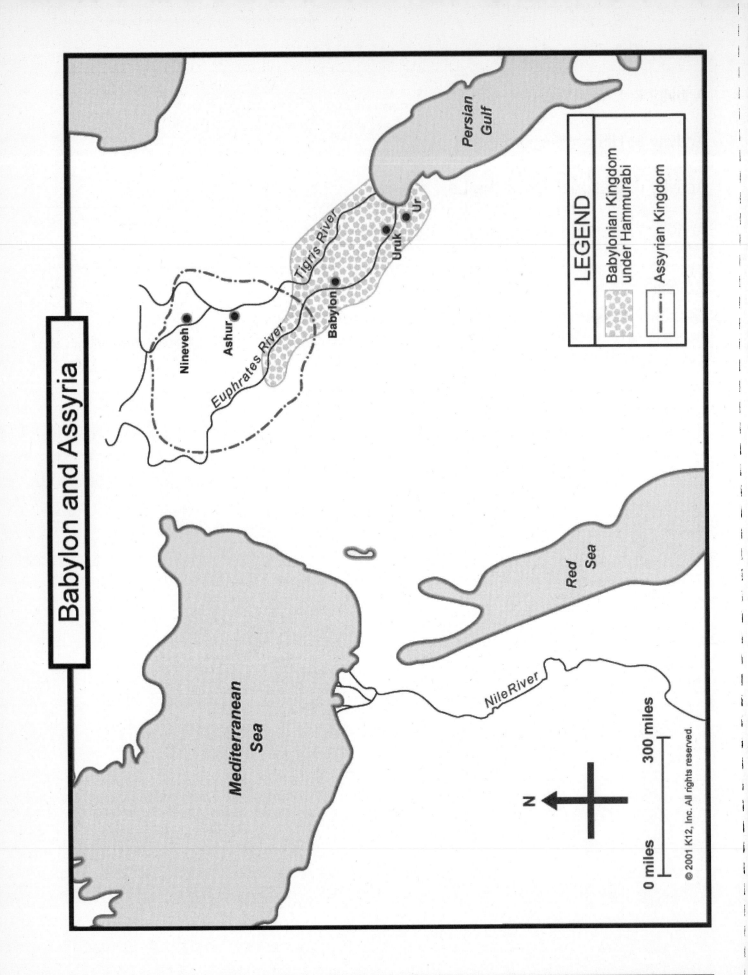

Babylon and Assyria

Persian
Gulf

Ur

Uruk

Tigris River

Babylon

Nineveh

Ashur

Euphrates River

LEGEND

Babylonian Kingdom
under Hammurabi

Assyrian Kingdom

Mediterranean
Sea

Red
Sea

Nile River

N

0 miles   300 miles

© 2001 K12, Inc. All rights reserved.

Lesson Assessment

Hammurabi, The Fair King

Short-Answer Questions:

1. What did Hammurabi write down on the stone monument?

2. What were these laws called?

3. Had any laws been written before these?

4. Why are laws important to a civilization?

Student Guide
Lesson 8: A Mesopotamian Myth: The Legend of Gilgamesh

Both the Babylonians and the Assyrians told stories about a king named Gilgamesh. Those stories have survived over the centuries and form one of the earliest works of literature.

Lesson Objectives

- Tell the main events from The Legend of Gilgamesh and Enkidu.

PREPARE

Approximate lesson time is 60 minutes.

Materials

For the Student

    🖥 map of Babylon and Assyria

    crayons, 16 or more

    pencils, no. 2

    paper, 8 1/2" x 11"

    brush, watercolor

    card stock

    Elmer's Glue-All

    glitter

    newspaper - or magazines

    paints, watercolor, 8 colors or more

    plastic wrap

    popsicle sticks

    scissors, round-end safety

    History Record Book

    paper, colored construction, 12"x12"

    markers, colored, 8 or more

    pencils, colored, 16 or more

Keywords and Pronunciation

Anu (AH-noo)

Enkidu (EN-kee-doo)

Gilgamesh (GIL-guh-mesh)

legend : An old story that may or may not be true.

trapper : A person who catches animals such as rabbits and foxes in traps and sells their fur to make money.

Uruk (OO-rouk)

LEARN
Activity 1: A Very Old Legend *(Online)*

Activity 2: The Legend of Gilgamesh *(Online)*

Activity 3: Show You Know *(Online)*

Activity 4: History Record Book *(Online)*

Activity 5. Optional: An Enkidu Mask *(Online)*

Activity 6. Optional: Gilgamesh and Enkidu Help Out *(Online)*

ASSESS
Lesson Assessment: A Mesopotamian Myth: The Legend of Gilgamesh *(Offline)*
You will complete an offline assessment covering the main objectives of this lesson. Your learning coach will score this assessment.

LEARN
Activity 7. Optional: Retell the Story *(Online)*

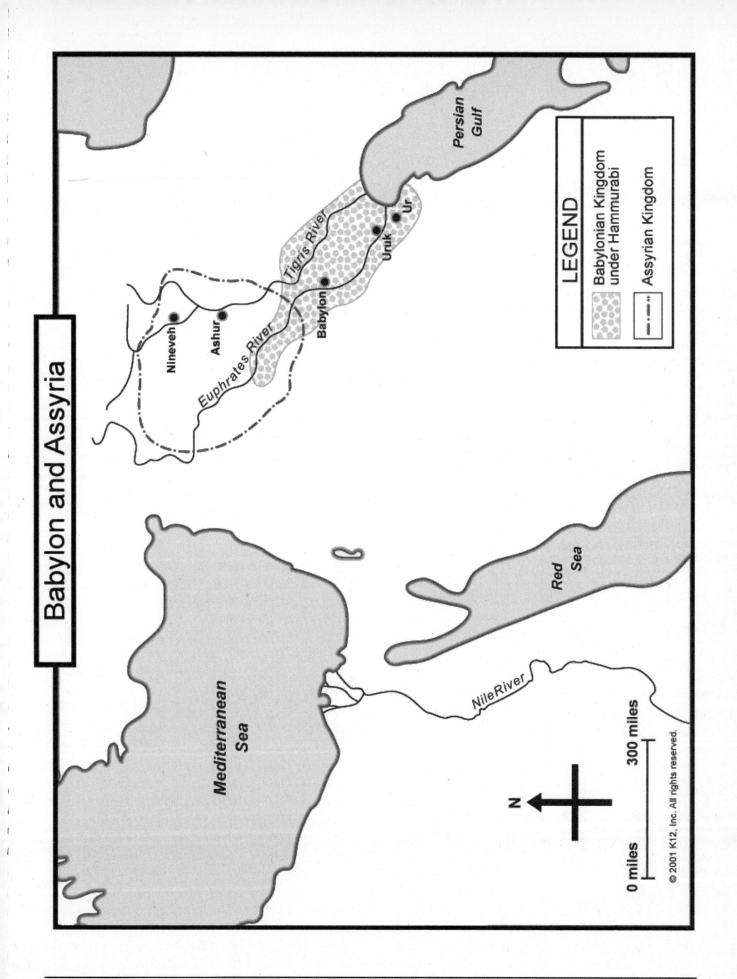

Babylon and Assyria

Persian Gulf

Tigris River

Ur

Uruk

Babylon

Euphrates River

Nineveh

Ashur

LEGEND

Babylonian Kingdom under Hammurabi

Assyrian Kingdom

Mediterranean Sea

Red Sea

Nile River

N

0 miles   300 miles

© 2001 K12, Inc. All rights reserved.

163

Name _____   Date _____

Lesson Assessment

A Mesopotamian Myth: The Legend of Gilgamesh

Short-Answer Question:

1. What are the main events of the story, The Legend of Gilgamesh and Enkidu?

Student Guide
Lesson 9: Rivers as Roads in Mesopotamia

Rivers not only made farming possible, they also served as "roads" to connect ancient peoples and allow them to trade with each other.

Lesson Objectives

- Demonstrate mastery of important knowledge and skills taught in this unit.
- Locate the Tigris River and the Euphrates River on a map.
- Demonstrate mastery of important knowledge and skills taught in previous lessons.
- Explain that monuments such as pyramids and ziggurats were built to honor the gods worshipped by people in ancient civilizations.
- Identify Mesopotamian temples as ziggurats.
- Explain why Abraham went to Canaan.
- Know that the followers of Judaism believe in one God.
- Identify Abraham's many descendants as the Israelites, or the Jewish people.
- Know that the Israelites left Canaan and went to Egypt.
- Identify Babylon as a large, powerful city in Mesopotamia.
- Identify the Code of Hammurabi as the first written set of laws.
- Tell the main events from The Legend of Gilgamesh and Enkidu.

PREPARE

Approximate lesson time is 60 minutes.

Materials

For the Student

- 🖥 map of Babylon and Assyria
- 🖥 Rivers as Roads activity sheet
- crayons, 16 or more
- 🖥 Land or River coloring sheet

LEARN
Activity 1: The Land of Mesopotamia (Online)

Activity 2: Reviewing Unit Three (Online)

ASSESS
Unit Assessment: The Rise of Ancient Empires (*Offline*)
Complete an offline Unit Assessment. Your learning coach will score this part of the Assessment.

LEARN
Activity 3. Optional: Rivers as Roads *(Online)*

Activity 4. Optional: River Roads and City Trade *(Online)*

Activity 5. Optional: Land or River? *(Online)*

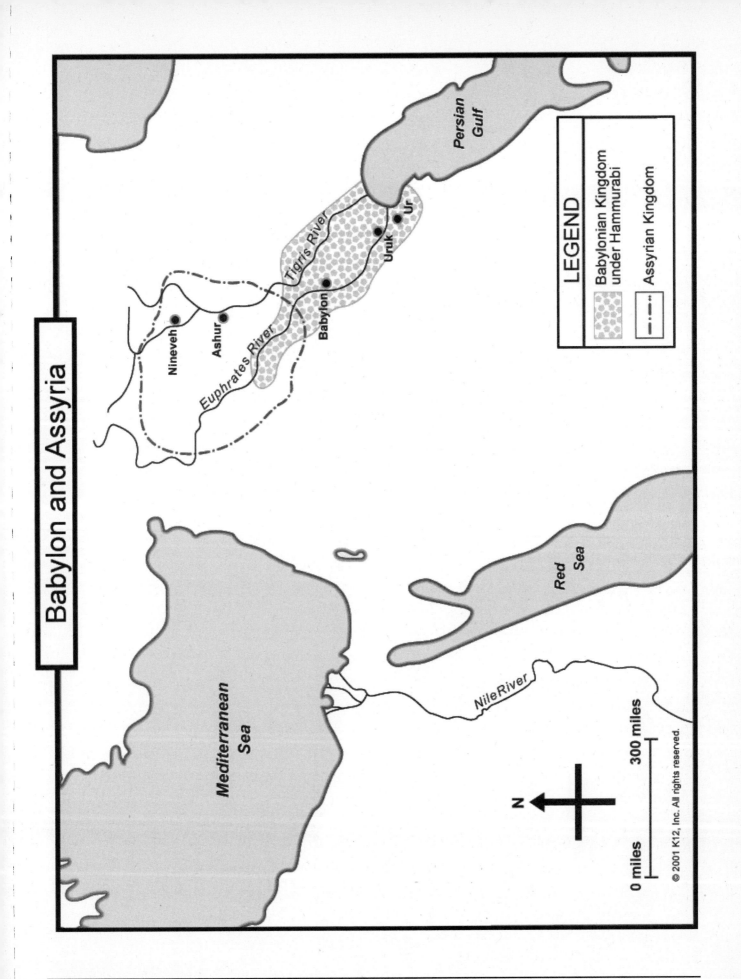

Babylon and Assyria

Persian Gulf

Tigris River

Ur

Uruk

Babylon

Euphrates River

Nineveh

Ashur

LEGEND

Babylonian Kingdom under Hammurabi

Assyrian Kingdom

Mediterranean Sea

Red Sea

Nile River

N

0 miles

300 miles

© 2001 K12, Inc. All rights reserved.

Name _____   Date _____

The Rise of Ancient Empires

Select the one best answer. Shade or color the bubble for the answer you choose.

1. Tall, stair-stepped monuments in ancient Mesopotamia are called

   _____.

   ○ pyramids
   ○ ziggurats
   ○ cuneiform

2. Egyptian pyramids and Mesopotamian ziggurats show that these ancient

   peoples were good at _____.

   ○ singing
   ○ building
   ○ poetry

3. I lived in Ur and traveled to Canaan. God told me to go there and worship

   only one God, not the many gods of Mesopotamia. Who am I?

   ○ Abraham
   ○ Sargon
   ○ Joseph

4. Abraham's descendents are called _____.

   ○ Egyptians
   ○ Jews
   ○ Babylonians

5. Where did the Israelites go when they left Canaan?
   - ○ Mesopotamia
   - ○ Babylon
   - ○ Egypt

6. Babylon was a large, powerful city in _____.
   - ○ Mesopotamia
   - ○ Egypt
   - ○ Canaan

7. Hammurabi was famous for writing _____.
   - ○ a book of poetry
   - ○ a story of gods
   - ○ a code of laws

8. Followers of Judaism believe in one God.
   - ○ True
   - ○ False

9. I am a king of ancient Mesopotamia who was taught a lesson by a monster named Enkidu. Who am I?
   - ○ Hammurabi
   - ○ Gilgamesh
   - ○ Abraham

Locate the following on the map of Mesopotamia.

10. Color Mesopotamia yellow.
11. Draw a red line for the Tigris River.
12. Draw a blue line for the Euphrates River.

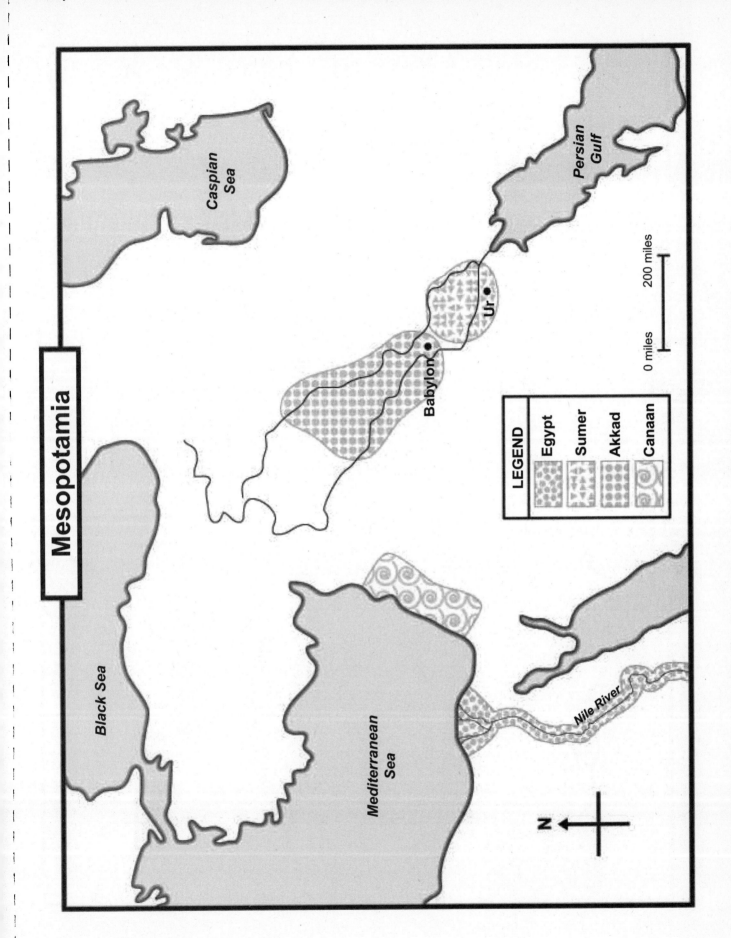

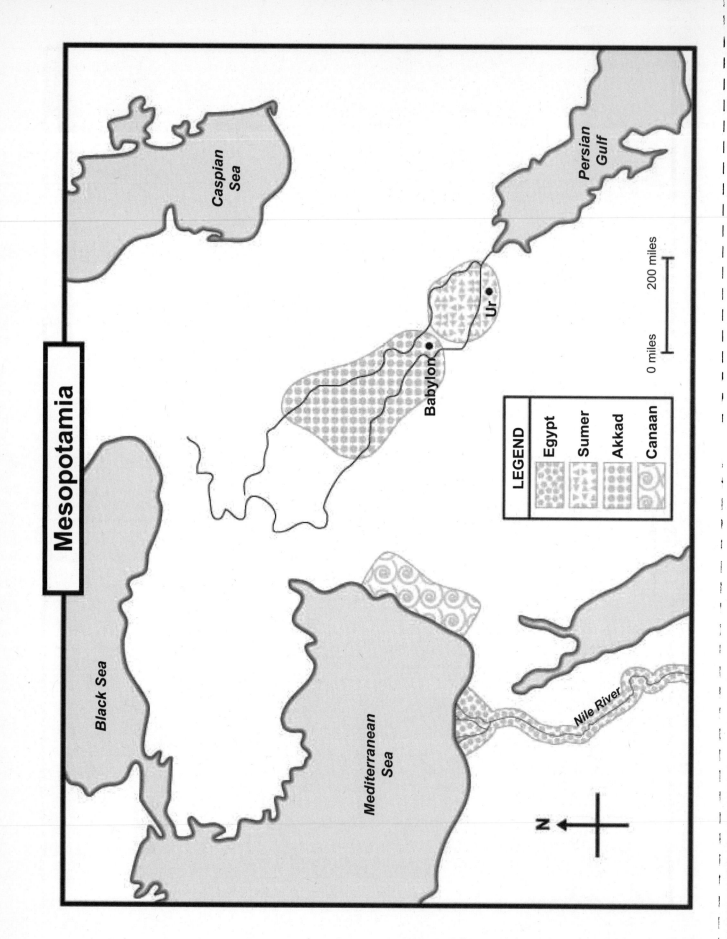

Mesopotamia

Caspian Sea

Persian Gulf

Ur

Babylon

200 miles

0 miles

LEGEND

Egypt

Sumer

Akkad

Canaan

Black Sea

Mediterranean Sea

Nile River

N

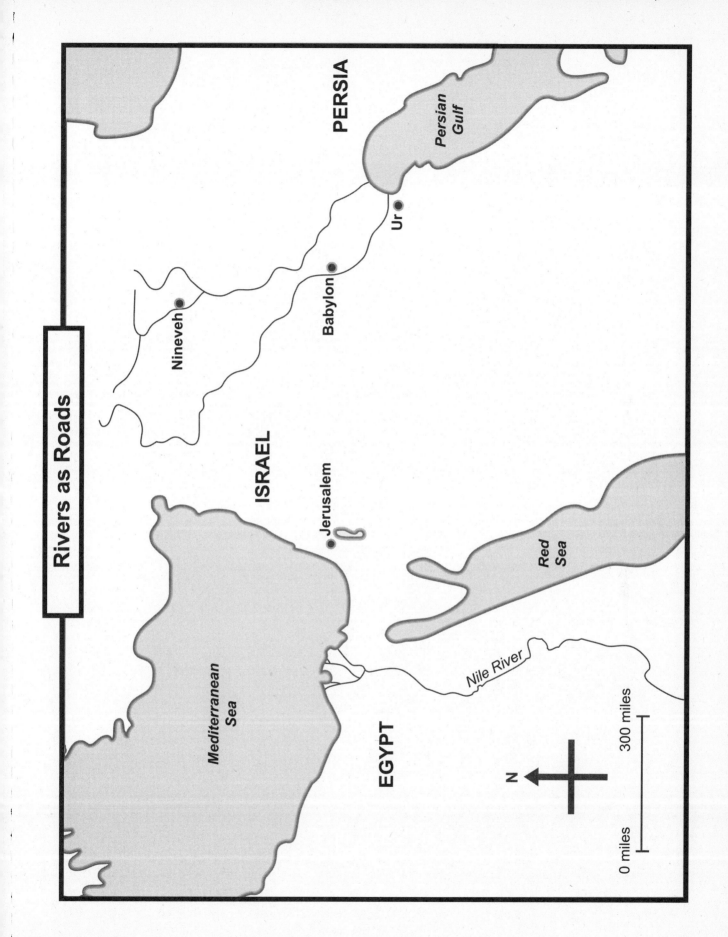

Rivers as Roads

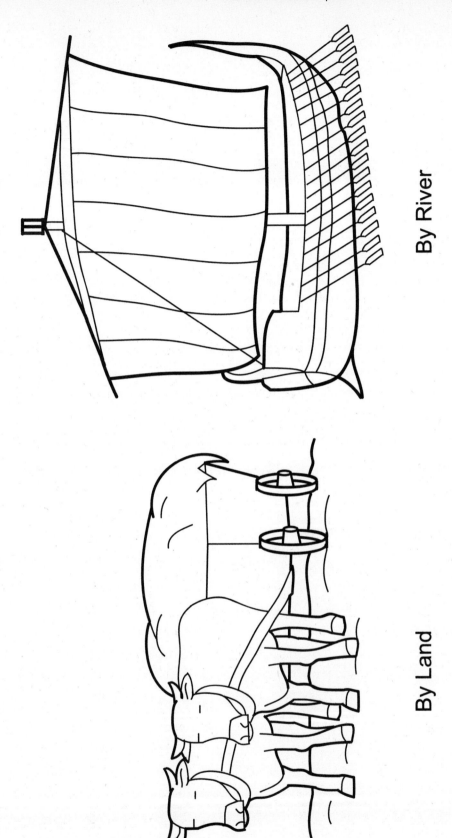

By River

By Land

Which form of transportation was faster? Why?

Student Guide
Lesson 1. Optional: Egypt Weak and Strong

Explore a strengthened Egypt, and meet two famous pharaohs. Learn about the Israelites' worship of one god, their flight from Egypt, and the leadership of Moses, David, and Solomon. Travel to Babylon to learn about a strong king who built one of the wonders of the ancient world.

Lesson Objectives

- Identify the Hyksos as invaders of ancient Egypt.
- Explain that the Hyksos brought horses to ancient Egypt.
- State that the Egyptians later defeated the Hyksos.

PREPARE

Approximate lesson time is 60 minutes.

Materials

For the Student

- map of Mesopotamia
- map of Ancient Egypt
  crayons, 16 or more
  pencils, no. 2
  paper, 8 1/2" x 11"
- Egyptian Charioteer coloring sheet
- What Did the Hyksos Bring?

Keywords and Pronunciation

chariot : An ancient two-wheeled vehicle pulled by horses.

Hyksos (HICK-sohs)

LEARN

Activity 1. Optional: Optional Lesson Instructions *(Online)*

This lesson is OPTIONAL. It is provided for students who seek enrichment or extra practice. You may skip this lesson.

If you choose to skip this lesson, then go to the Plan or Lesson Lists page and mark this lesson "Skipped" in order to proceed to the next lesson in the course.

Activity 2. Optional: Finding Places *(Online)*

Activity 3. Optional: The Strong Begin to Fall *(Online)*

Activity 4. Optional: The Strength of the Hyksos *(Online)*

Activity 5. Optional: Show You Know *(Online)*

Activity 6. Optional: History Record Book *(Online)*

Activity 7. Optional: Egyptian Charioteer *(Online)*

Activity 8. Optional: What the Hyksos Brought *(Online)*

Activity 9. Optional: Ancient Egypt and Now *(Online)*

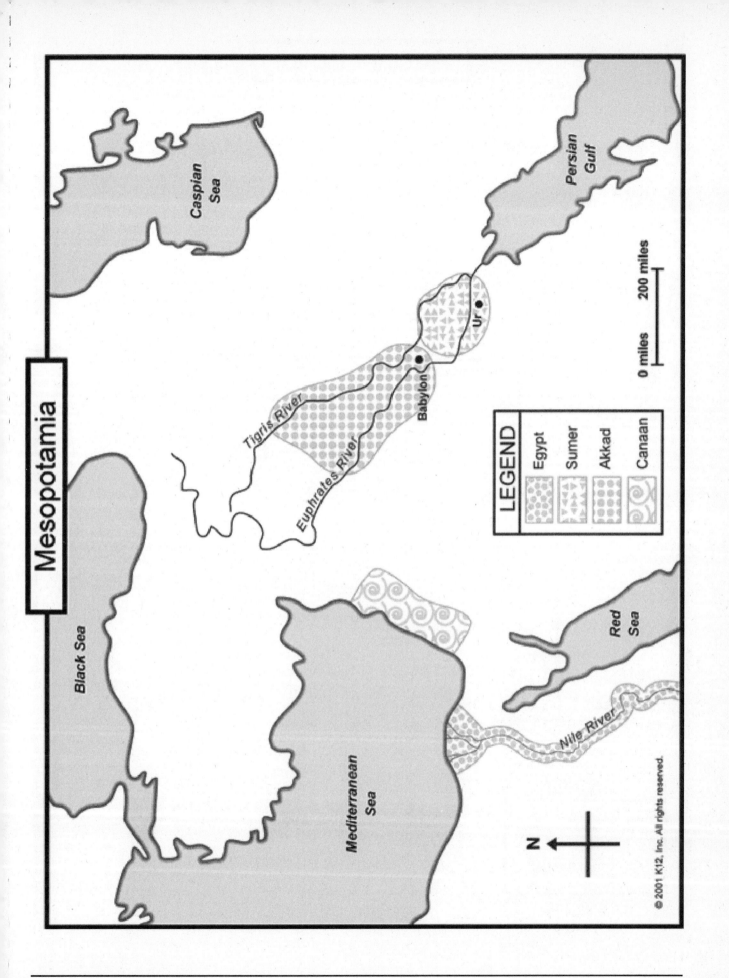

Mesopotamia

Black Sea

Caspian Sea

Persian Gulf

Tigris River

Euphrates River

Babylon

Ur

Mediterranean Sea

Red Sea

Nile River

LEGEND
Egypt
Sumer
Akkad
Canaan

0 miles   200 miles

N

© 2001 K12, Inc. All rights reserved.

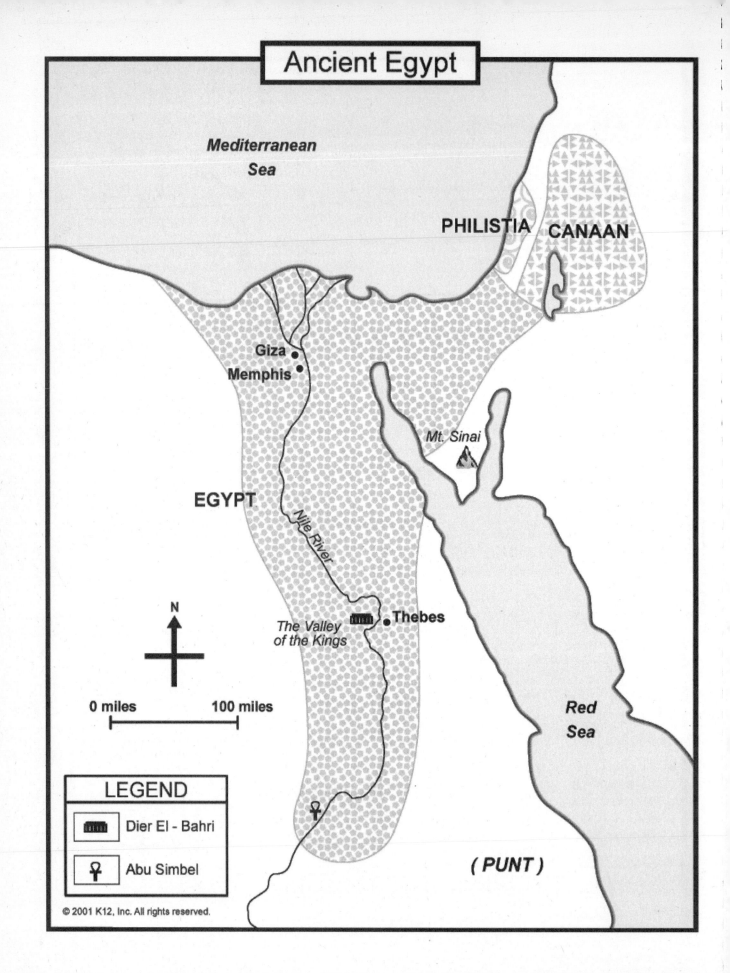

Ancient Egypt

Mediterranean Sea

PHILISTIA CANAAN

Giza
Memphis

EGYPT

Nile River

Mt. Sinai

N

The Valley of the Kings

Thebes

Red Sea

0 miles   100 miles

LEGEND

Dier El - Bahri

Abu Simbel

(PUNT)

Pharaoh on Chariot

Name _____   Date _____

What Did the Hyksos Bring?

Circle the item the Hyksos bring to Egypt that helped them defeat the Egyptians.

Student Guide
Lesson 2: A Woman as Pharaoh!

Hatshepsut was one of the only women to rule Egypt. She ordered the exploration of new lands and the building of a great temple, wherein we can find the record of what happened during her peaceful and prosperous reign.

Lesson Objectives
- Explain that Hatshepsut left a record of her reign behind in a great temple.
- Identify Hatshepsut as one of the few women who ruled as pharaoh of ancient Egypt.

PREPARE

Approximate lesson time is 60 minutes.

Materials
For the Student
- map, world
- map of Ancient Egypt
- crayons, 16 or more
- Show You Know
- pencils, no. 2
- paper, 8 1/2" x 11"
- paper, colored construction, 12"x12"
- brush, watercolor
- paints, watercolor, 8 colors or more
- toilet paper tubes
- markers, dry-erase
- string

Keywords and Pronunciation
Deir el-Bahri (dehr el-BAH-ree)
Hatshepsut (Hat-SHEP-soot)
lapis lazuli (LAP-uhs LA-zuh-lee)
myrrh (muhr)
Punt (poont)

LEARN

Activity 1: Question and Answer *(Online)*

Activity 2: The Story of Hatshepsut *(Online)*

Activity 3: The Route to Punt *(Online)*

Activity 4: Show You Know *(Online)*

Activity 5: History Record Book *(Online)*

ASSESS

Lesson Assessment: A Woman as Pharaoh! (*Offline*)

You will complete an offline assessment covering the main objectives of this lesson. Your learning coach will score this assessment.

LEARN

Activity 6. Optional: Tomb Painter for Hatshepsut *(Online)*

Activity 7. Optional: Make a Beard *(Online)*

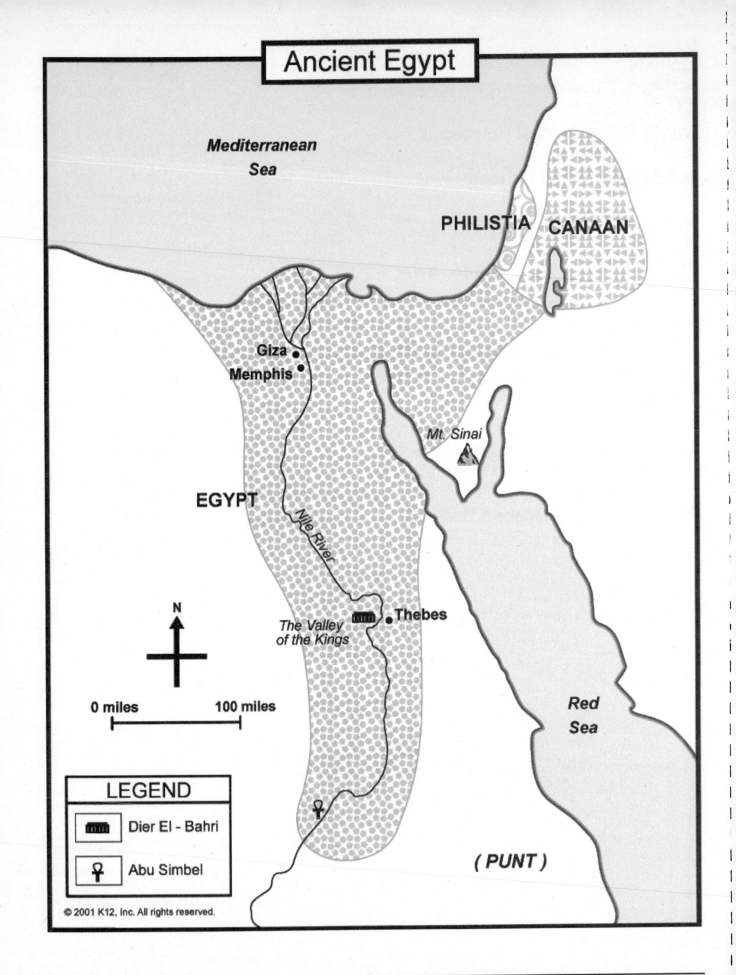

Ancient Egypt

Mediterranean
Sea

PHILISTIA   CANAAN

Giza
Memphis

EGYPT

Nile River

Mt. Sinai

N

The Valley
of the Kings

Thebes

0 miles   100 miles

Red
Sea

LEGEND

Dier El - Bahri

Abu Simbel

(PUNT)

Show You Know

A Woman as Pharaoh!

Short-Answer Questions:

Enter Answers here

1. Were most of the pharaohs of ancient Egypt men or women?

2. Name one woman who ruled as a pharaoh of ancient Egypt.

3. Can you tell me one thing Hatshepsut did while she was pharaoh?

4. How do we know what happened while Hatshepsut was pharaoh?

Name _____ Date _____

Lesson Assessment

A Woman as Pharaoh!

Short-Answer Questions:

1. Name one woman who ruled as a pharaoh of ancient Egypt.

2. How do we know what happened while Hatshepsut was pharaoh?

Student Guide
Lesson 3: Ramses II: The Great Builder

Pharaoh Ramses II was the greatest builder in Egypt's history. Of all the temples, statues, and other buildings credited to him today, the most famous is the Great Temple of Abu Simbel. This temple was carved into a cliff in southern Egypt.

Lesson Objectives

- Name Ramses II as the pharaoh who ordered the building of many temples and statues.
- Identify Abu Simbel as a temple built by Ramses II.

PREPARE

Approximate lesson time is 60 minutes.

Materials

For the Student

    📖 map of Ancient Egypt

    crayons, 16 or more

    clay, colored

    paper, colored construction, 12"x12"

    markers, colored, 8 or more

    pencils, no. 2

    paper, 8 1/2" x 11"

    📖 Abu Simbel activity sheet

    Play-Doh

    blocks - building

    paper, drawing, 12" x 18"

Keywords and Pronunciation

Abu Simbel (ah-boo SIM-bel)

Ramses (RAM-seez)

LEARN
Activity 1: The Egyptian People *(Online)*

Activity 2: Discovering Ramses *(Online)*

Activity 3: Show You Know *(Online)*

Activity 4: History Record Book *(Online)*

Activity 5. Optional: Who Is It? *(Online)*

Activity 6. Optional: Making a Statue *(Online)*

ASSESS

Lesson Assessment: Ramses II: The Great Builder *(Online)*

You will complete an offline assessment covering the main objectives of this lesson. Your learning coach will score this assessment.

LEARN

Activity 7. Optional: Exploring Abu Simbel *(Online)*

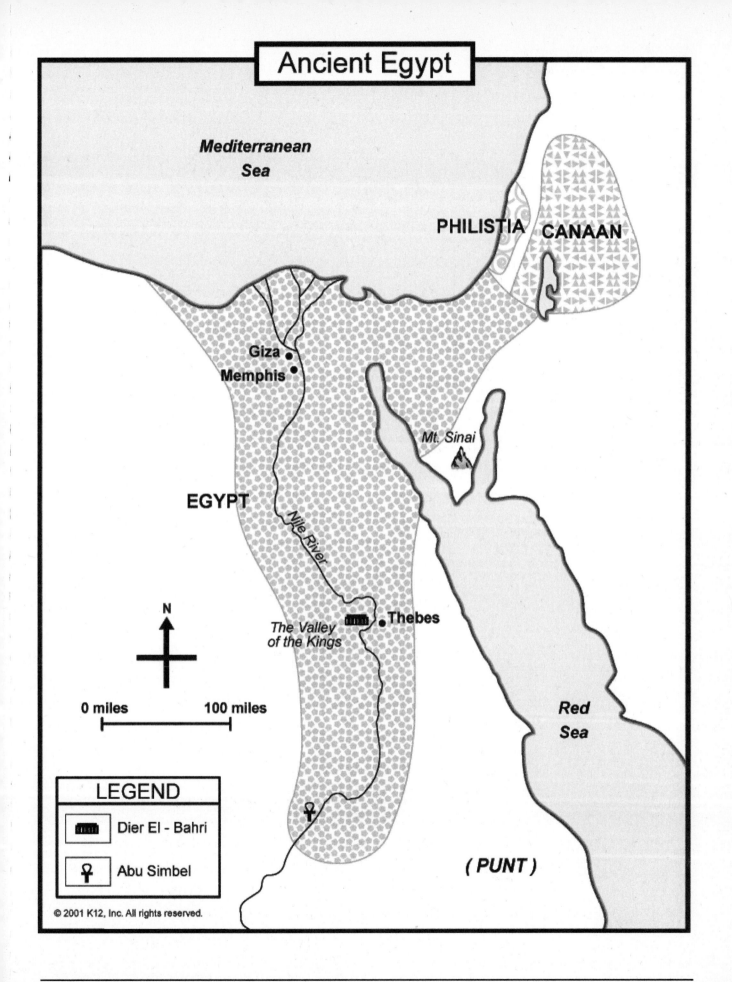

Ancient Egypt

Mediterranean
Sea

PHILISTIA   CANAAN

Giza
Memphis

Mt. Sinai

EGYPT

Nile River

N

The Valley
of the Kings

Thebes

0 miles   100 miles

Red
Sea

LEGEND

Dier El - Bahri

Abu Simbel

(PUNT)

© 2001 K12, Inc. All rights reserved.

Name _____   Date _____

Lesson Assessment

Ramses II: The Great Builder

Short-Answer Questions:

1. What is the name of the Egyptian pharaoh in this story who ordered the building of many temples and statues?

2. What is the name of the temple he built in the cliff?

Student Guide
Lesson 4: Moses in the Basket

Learn more about the history of the Israelites, beginning with their enslavement by the Egyptians. In this lesson your student will hear the first half of a Bible story about a leader who would eventually deliver the Israelites from their captivity--Moses.

Lesson Objectives

- State that the Israelites worshipped one god.
- Explain that the Israelites went to Egypt and were enslaved by the Egyptians.
- Identify Moses as a Jew who was raised as an Egyptian.

PREPARE

Approximate lesson time is 60 minutes.

Materials

For the Student

     📖 Abraham's Family Tree

     📖 map of Ancient Egypt

     pencils, colored, 16 or more

     📖 Show You Know

     crayons, 16 or more

     pencils, no. 2

     paper, 8 1/2" x 11"

     paper, colored construction, 12"x12"

     markers, colored, 8 or more

     📖 Footprints from Canaan to Egypt activity sheet

     glue sticks

     scissors, round-end safety

Keywords and Pronunciation

enslave : To make someone a slave.

famine : A shortage of food.

LEARN
Activity 1: Review Narration *(Online)*

Activity 2: Egyptians and Israelites *(Online)*

Activity 3: Moses in the Basket *(Online)*

Activity 4: Show You Know *(Online)*

Activity 5: History Record Book *(Online)*

Activity 6. Optional: Storyboard *(Online)*

Activity 7. Optional: Footprints from Canaan to Egypt *(Online)*

ASSESS

Lesson Assessment: Moses in the Basket (*Offline*)

You will complete an offline assessment covering the main objectives of this lesson. Your learning coach will score this assessment.

LEARN

Activity 8. Optional: Escaping Famine *(Online)*

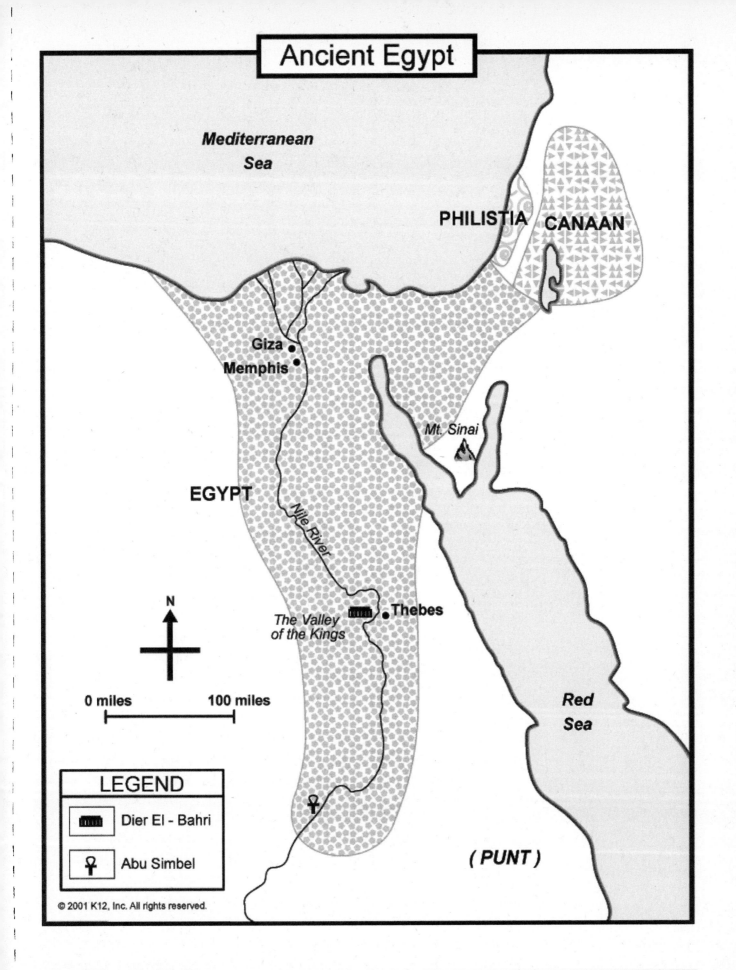

Ancient Egypt

Mediterranean Sea

PHILISTIA CANAAN

Giza
Memphis

EGYPT

Nile River

Mt. Sinai

The Valley
of the Kings

Thebes

N

0 miles   100 miles

Red
Sea

LEGEND

Dier El - Bahri

Abu Simbel

(PUNT)

203

Children of Israel

Jacob's Sons

Jacob

Isaac

Abraham and Sarah

Show You Know

Moses in the Basket

Short-Answer Questions:

Enter Answers here

1. Who were the Israelites descended from?

2. Did the Israelites worship one God or many gods?

3. Why did the Israelites go to Egypt?

4. What happened to them in Egypt?

5. What terrible command did the Pharaoh give?

6. Which Jewish boy was not killed and was raised as an Egyptian?

7. What did Moses' mother do to keep him from being killed?

Name _____ Date _____

Footprints From Canaan to Egypt

Read the sentences below. Then put them in the best order to show the path of the Israelites from Canaan to Egypt.

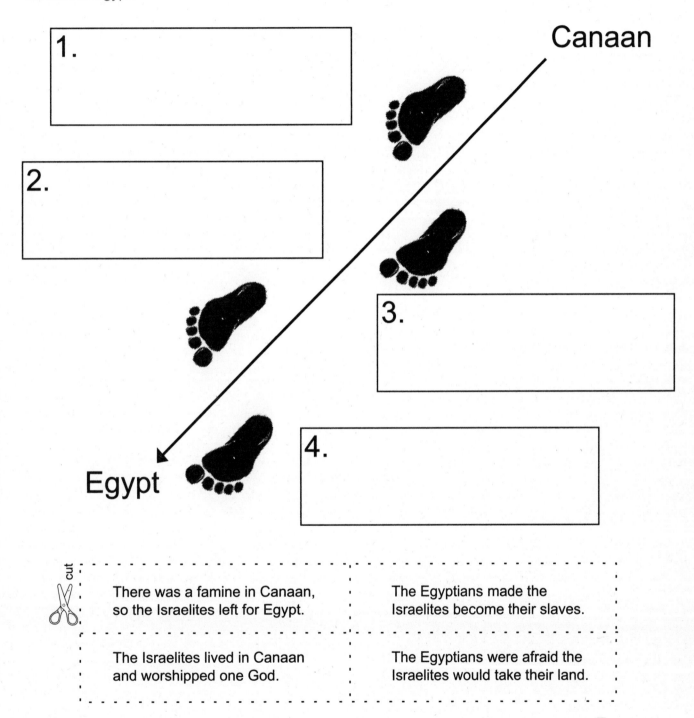

Canaan

1.

2.

3.

4.

Egypt

cut ✂

There was a famine in Canaan, so the Israelites left for Egypt.	The Egyptians made the Israelites become their slaves.
The Israelites lived in Canaan and worshipped one God.	The Egyptians were afraid the Israelites would take their land.

Lesson Assessment

Moses in the Basket

Short-Answer Questions:

1. Did the Israelites worship one God or many gods?

2. Why did the Israelites go to Egypt?

3. What happened to the Israelites in Egypt?

4. Which Jewish boy was not killed and was raised as an Egyptian?

Student Guide
Lesson 5: The Exodus from Egypt

Lesson Objectives

- Identify Moses as the man who led the Israelites out of Egypt.
- Name Exodus as the Israelites' long journey out of Egypt.

PREPARE

Approximate lesson time is 60 minutes.

Materials

For the Student

crayons, 16 or more

pencils, no. 2

paper, 8 1/2" x 11"

🖻 Ancient Egypt location map

🖻 Exodus Events Activity Sheet

glue sticks

scissors, round-end safety

Exodus by Brian Wildsmith

Keywords and Pronunciation

Exodus (EK-suh-duhs) : The Israelites´ long journey out of Egypt.

LEARN
Activity 1: A Quick Review *(Online)*

Activity 2: The Exodus from Egypt *(Online)*

Activity 3: The Exodus from Egypt *(Online)*

Activity 4: History Record Book *(Online)*

Activity 5. Optional: Where Did it Happen? *(Online)*

Activity 6. Optional: Act It Out (Online)

ASSESS
Lesson Assessment: The Exodus from Egypt (*Offline*)
You will complete an offline assessment covering the main objectives of this lesson. Your learning coach will score this assessment.

LEARN
Activity 7. Optional: The Story of the Exodus (Online)

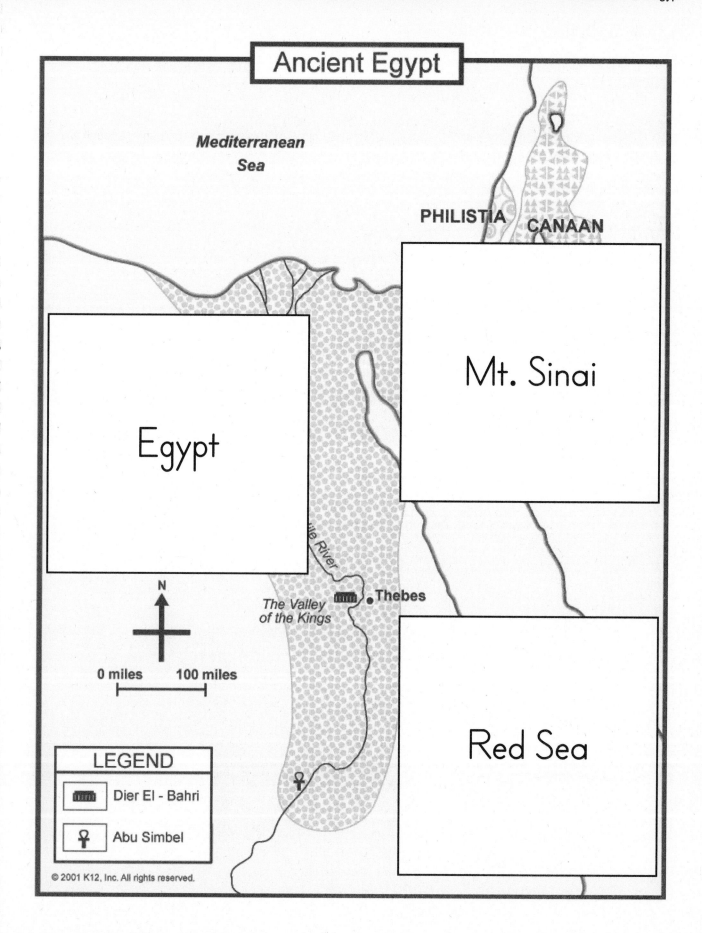

Ancient Egypt

Mediterranean Sea

PHILISTIA   CANAAN

Mt. Sinai

Egypt

N

0 miles   100 miles

The Valley of the Kings

Nile River

Dier El - Bahri   Thebes

Red Sea

LEGEND

Dier El - Bahri

Abu Simbel

© 2001 K12, Inc. All rights reserved.

Exodus Events

Identify and summarize the three events depicted on the sheet. Color the drawings, cut them out, and glue them in their correct locations on the Ancient Egypt location map.

✂ cut

Lesson Assessment

The Exodus from Egypt

Short-Answer Questions:

1. Who led the Israelites out of Egypt?

2. What do we call the Israelites' long journey out of Egypt?

Student Guide
Lesson 6: David, Israel's Second King

Learn more about the Israelites after Moses led them out of slavery in Egypt back to Canaan. There, the Israelites chose their first king, Saul. And after Saul, David became king. In this lesson your student will hear the famous story of David and Goliath.

Lesson Objectives

- Identify the land of Canaan as the new home for the nation of Israel.
- Identify Saul as the first king of Israel.
- Retell main events from the story of David and Goliath.

PREPARE

Approximate lesson time is 60 minutes.

Materials

For the Student

    🖳 map of Ancient Egypt

    crayons, 16 or more

    pencils, no. 2

    Tales from the Old Testament, CD by Jim Weiss

    🖳 Show You Know

    paper, 8 1/2" x 11"

    paper, colored construction, 12"x12"

    pencils, colored, 16 or more

    clay, colored

    markers, colored, 8 or more

    paper clips

Keywords and Pronunciation

Philistines (FIH-luh-steens)

LEARN
Activity 1: Led by Moses *(Online)*

Activity 2: King of Israel *(Online)*

Activity 3: David and Goliath *(Online)*

Activity 4: Show You Know *(Online)*

Activity 5: History Record Book *(Online)*

Activity 6. Optional: David Versus Goliath *(Online)*

ASSESS

Lesson Assessment: David, Israel's Second King (*Offline*)

You will complete an offline assessment covering the main objectives of this lesson. Your learning coach will score this assessment.

LEARN

Activity 7. Optional: Goliath the Giant *(Online)*

Activity 8. Optional: Read On *(Online)*

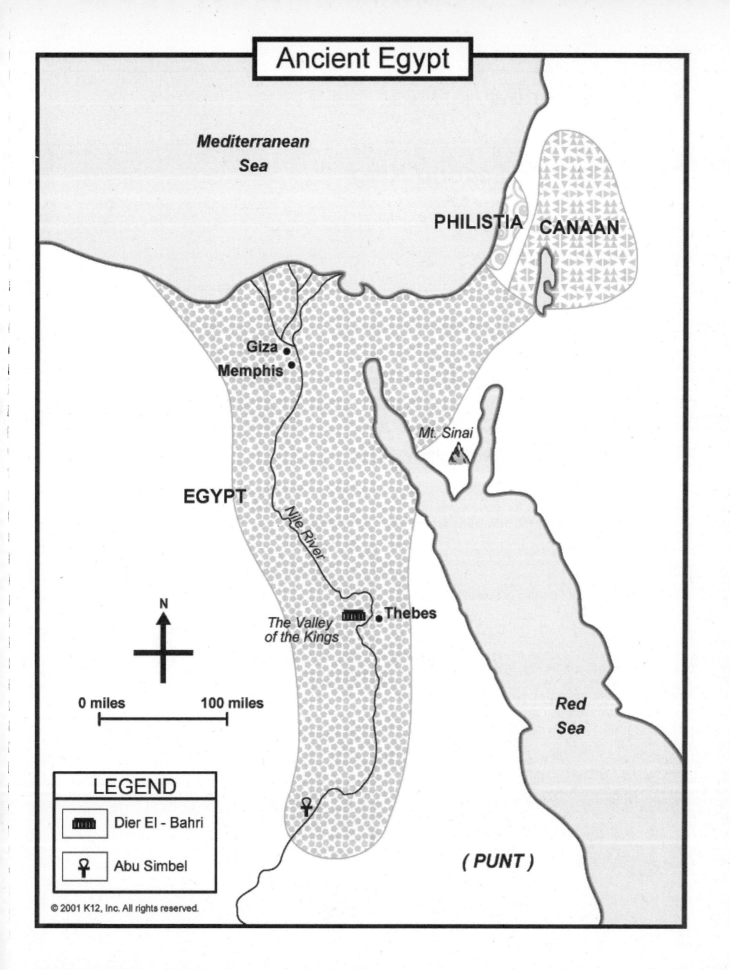

Ancient Egypt

Mediterranean Sea

PHILISTIA   CANAAN

Giza
Memphis

Mt. Sinai

EGYPT

Nile River

N

The Valley
of the Kings

Thebes

Red
Sea

0 miles   100 miles

LEGEND

Dier El - Bahri

Abu Simbel

(PUNT)

Name _____ Date _____

Show You Know

David, Israel's Second King

Short-Answer Questions:

Enter Answers here

1. Tell me what you know about the story of David and Goliath. Who won the battle between David and Goliath?

2. What weapon did David use to bring down Goliath?

3. Were you surprised that David defeated Goliath? Why?

4. What land became the new home for the nation of Israel?

5. Who was the first king of Israel?

6. Who became the king after Saul?

Name _____ Date _____

Lesson Assessment

David, Israel's Second King

Short-Answer Questions:

1. Who was the first king of Israel?

2. What land became the new home for the nation of Israel?

3. What do you know about the story of David and Goliath?

Student Guide
Lesson 7: Solomon, the Wise King

After the reign of King David, the Israelites enjoyed a time of relative peace and strength under the rule of wise King Solomon. Today, hear a famous story about how Solomon used his wisdom to make a difficult decision.

Lesson Objectives

- Tell that Solomon was considered a wise king because he was able to solve difficult problems.
- Identify Solomon as the king of Israel who followed David.

PREPARE

Approximate lesson time is 60 minutes.

Materials

For the Student

   Tales from the Old Testament, CD by Jim Weiss

   🖳 Show You Know

   crayons, 16 or more

   pencils, no. 2

   paper, 8 1/2" x 11"

   paper, colored construction, 12"x12"

   pencils, colored, 16 or more

   markers, colored, 8 or more

   scissors, round-end safety

   King Solomon and His Magic Ring by Elie Wiesel

   King Solomon and the Queen of Sheba by Blu Greenberg

Keywords and Pronunciation

wisdom : Knowledge and good judgment.

LEARN
Activity 1: Israel's First Kings *(Online)*

Activity 2: A Wise King *(Online)*

Activity 3: Show You Know *(Online)*

Activity 4: History Record Book *(Online)*

Activity 5. Optional: Thank You, King Solomon *(Online)*

___

ASSESS

Lesson Assessment: Solomon, the Wise King (*Offline*)

You will complete an offline assessment covering the main objectives of this lesson. Your learning coach will score this assessment.

___

LEARN

Activity 6. Optional: Flip Through the Story *(Online)*

Activity 7. Optional: Optional Books *(Online)*

Name _____   Date _____

Show You Know

Solomon, the Wise King

Short-Answer Questions:

Enter Answers here

1. Saul was the first king of Israel. David was the second king. Who was the third king of Israel?

2. What does the name *Solomon* mean?

3. King Solomon was a wise king because he could do what?

4. In the story you heard about Solomon, what did he wish for?

5. In the story, why were the two women arguing?

6. Did King Solomon really mean it when he ordered that the baby be cut in half?

Name _____ Date _____

Lesson Assessment

Solomon, the Wise King

Short-Answer Questions:

1. Saul was the first king of Israel. David was the second king. Who was the third king of Israel?

2. King Solomon was a wise king because he could do what?

Student Guide
Lesson 8. Optional: The Warrior Who Built a Library

New military tactics made Assyria, for a time, the strongest empire in ancient Mesopotamia. Assyrian culture reached its height under Ashurbanipal. He collected oral tales, histories, and records on clay tablets, and stored them in a great library.

Lesson Objectives

- Tell that Ashurbanipal filled his library with clay tablets.
- State that Ashurbanipal was able to read and that he created one of the great libraries of the ancient world.
- Identify Assyria as a great empire in ancient Mesopotamia.
- Describe Ashurbanipal and the Assyrians as fierce, cruel, and innovative warriors.

PREPARE

Approximate lesson time is 60 minutes.

Materials

For the Student

    📖 map of the Assyrian Empire

    crayons, 16 or more

    pencils, no. 2

    paper, 8 1/2" x 11"

    clay, colored

    📖 map of Mesopotamia

    markers, colored, 8 or more

    paper, colored construction, 12"x12"

    scissors, round-end safety

    stapler

Keywords and Pronunciation

Ashurbanipal (ah-shur-BAN-nuh-pahl)

Nineveh (NIN-eh-vuh)

LEARN
Activity 1. Optional: Optional Lesson Instructions *(Online)*

This lesson is OPTIONAL. It is provided for students who seek enrichment or extra practice. You may skip this lesson.

If you choose to skip this lesson, then go to the Plan or Lesson Lists page and mark this lesson "Skipped" in order to proceed to the next lesson in the course.

Activity 2. Optional: Map Review *(Online)*

Activity 3. Optional: Locating Assyria *(Online)*

Activity 4. Optional: The Rise of Assyria *(Online)*

Activity 5. Optional: Show You Know *(Online)*

Activity 6. Optional: History Record Book *(Online)*

Activity 7. Optional: Clay Tablet *(Online)*

Activity 8. Optional: Color Maps *(Online)*

Activity 9. Optional: An Assyrian Shield *(Online)*

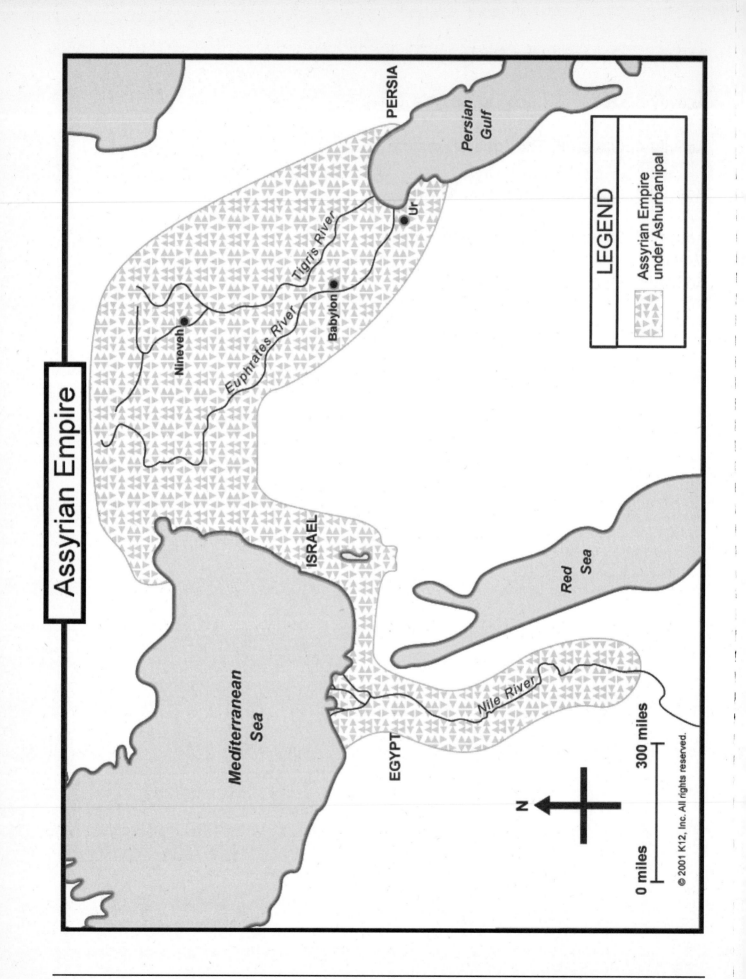

Assyrian Empire

LEGEND

Assyrian Empire under Ashurbanipal

PERSIA

Persian Gulf

Ur

Tigris River

Babylon

Euphrates River

Nineveh

ISRAEL

Mediterranean Sea

Red Sea

Nile River

EGYPT

N

0 miles   300 miles

© 2001 K12, Inc. All rights reserved.

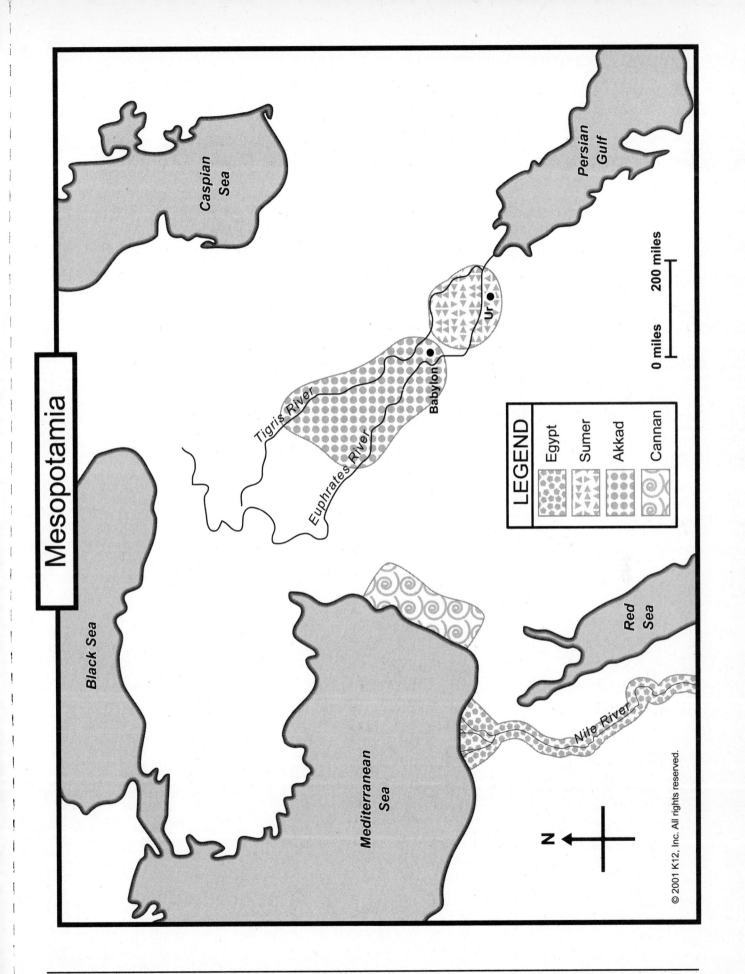

Mesopotamia

Caspian Sea

Persian Gulf

200 miles

0 miles

Tigris River

Babylon

Ur

Euphrates River

LEGEND

Egypt

Sumer

Akkad

Cannan

Black Sea

Red Sea

Mediterranean Sea

Nile River

N

© 2001 K12, Inc. All rights reserved.

Student Guide
Lesson 9: Back to Babylon

Nebuchadnezzar, Babylon's most famous king, restored the city of Babylon to its ancient glory and built one of the Seven Wonders of the Ancient World, the Hanging Gardens of Babylon.

Lesson Objectives

- Identify Nebuchadnezzar as a strong king of ancient Babylon.
- Identify Nebuchadnezzar as the king who built the Hanging Gardens of Babylon.
- Identify the Hanging Gardens of Babylon as one of the Seven Wonders of the Ancient World.

PREPARE

Approximate lesson time is 60 minutes.

Materials

For the Student

 map of the Babylonian Empire

 Show You Know

crayons, 16 or more

pencils, no. 2

paper, 8 1/2" x 11"

 Hanging Gardens of Babylon coloring sheet

markers, colored, 8 or more

pebbles

plastic wrap

rocks

The Revenge of Ishtar retold by Ludmila Zeman

Keywords and Pronunciation

Ishtar (ISH-tahr)

Nebuchadnezzar (neb-yuh-kud-NEH-zur)

Persia (PUR-zhuh)

LEARN
Activity 1: Babylon's Great Kings *(Online)*

Activity 2: King Nebuchadnezzar (Online)

Activity 3: Show You Know (Online)

Activity 4: History Record Book (Online)

Activity 5. Optional: Hanging Gardens Coloring Sheet (Online)

ASSESS
Lesson Assessment: Back to Babylon (*Offline*)
You will complete an offline assessment covering the main objectives of this lesson. Your learning coach will score this assessment.

LEARN
Activity 6. Optional: Build the Hanging Gardens (Online)

Activity 7. Optional: A Story of Gilgamesh and Ishtar (Online)

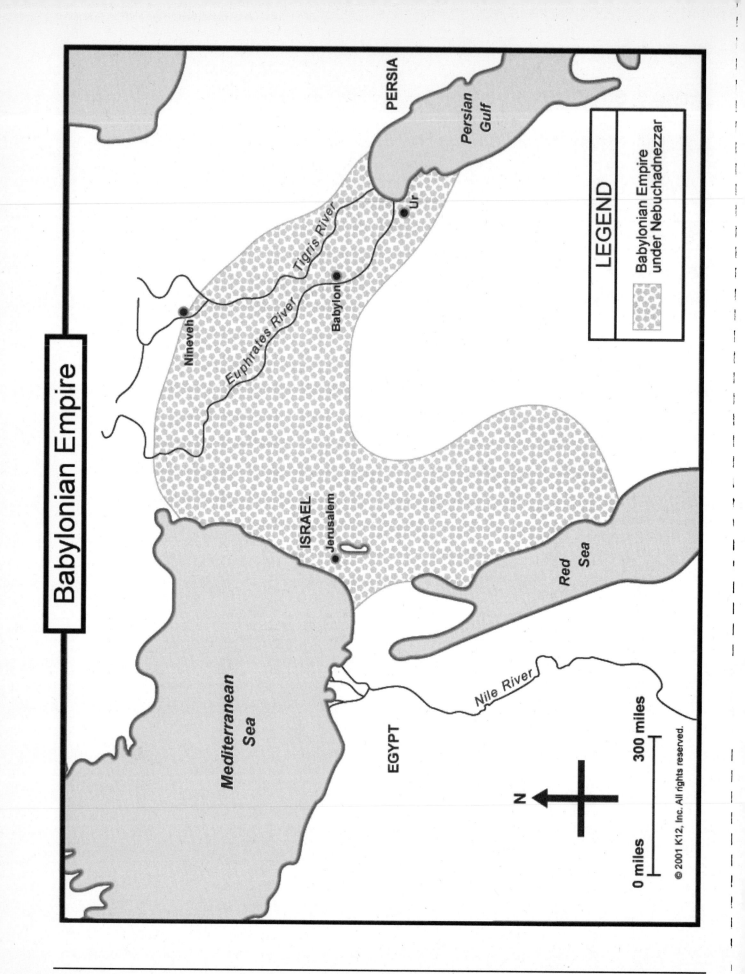

Babylonian Empire

LEGEND

Babylonian Empire under Nebuchadnezzar

PERSIA

Persian Gulf

Ur

Tigris River

Babylon

Euphrates River

Nineveh

ISRAEL

Jerusalem

Red Sea

Mediterranean Sea

EGYPT

Nile River

N

0 miles

300 miles

© 2001 K12, Inc. All rights reserved.

Show You Know

Back to Babylon

Short-Answer Questions:

Enter Answers here

1. Who was Nebuchadnezzar?

2. Why was Nebuchadnezzar afraid of Persia?

3. What did Nebuchadnezzar do to make sure Persia wouldn't attack Babylon?

4. Why was Amytis homesick in Babylon?

5. What did Nebuchadnezzar build to make Amytis happy?

6. We've learned about two of the Seven Wonders of the Ancient World. What are they?

Name _____   Date _____

Lesson Assessment

Back to Babylon

Short-Answer Questions:

1. Who was Nebuchadnezzar?

2. What did Nebuchadnezzar build to make Amytis happy?

3. Name two of the Seven Wonders of the Ancient World.

Student Guide
Lesson 10: Ishtar and Tammuz: A Babylonian Myth

Lesson Objectives

- Demonstrate mastery of important knowledge and skills taught in this unit.
- Demonstrate mastery of important knowledge and skills taught in previous lessons.
- Identify Hatshepsut as one of the few women who ruled as pharaoh of ancient Egypt.
- Name Ramses II as the pharaoh who ordered the building of many temples and statues.
- State that the Israelites worshipped one god.
- Identify Moses as a Jew who was raised as an Egyptian.
- Name Exodus as the Israelites' long journey out of Egypt.
- Identify Saul as the first king of Israel.
- Retell main events from the story of David and Goliath.
- Tell that Solomon was considered a wise king because he was able to solve difficult problems.
- Identify Solomon as the king of Israel who followed David.
- Identify Nebuchadnezzar as the king who built the Hanging Gardens of Babylon.

PREPARE

Approximate lesson time is 60 minutes.

Materials

For the Student

- 🖥 map of Babylonian Empire
- 🖥 Tammuz Returns coloring sheet
- crayons, 16 or more

Keywords and Pronunciation

Ishtar (ISH-tahr)

Tammuz (TAH-mouz)

LEARN
Activity 1: Looking Back *(Online)*

Activity 2: Reviewing Unit Four *(Online)*

ASSESS
Unit Assessment: Ancient Kingdoms Rise and Fall (*Offline*)
Complete an offline Unit Assessment. Your learning coach will score this part of the Assessment.

LEARN
Activity 3. Optional: Ishtar and Tammuz (*Online*)

Activity 4. Optional: Tammuz Returns (*Online*)

Babylonian Empire

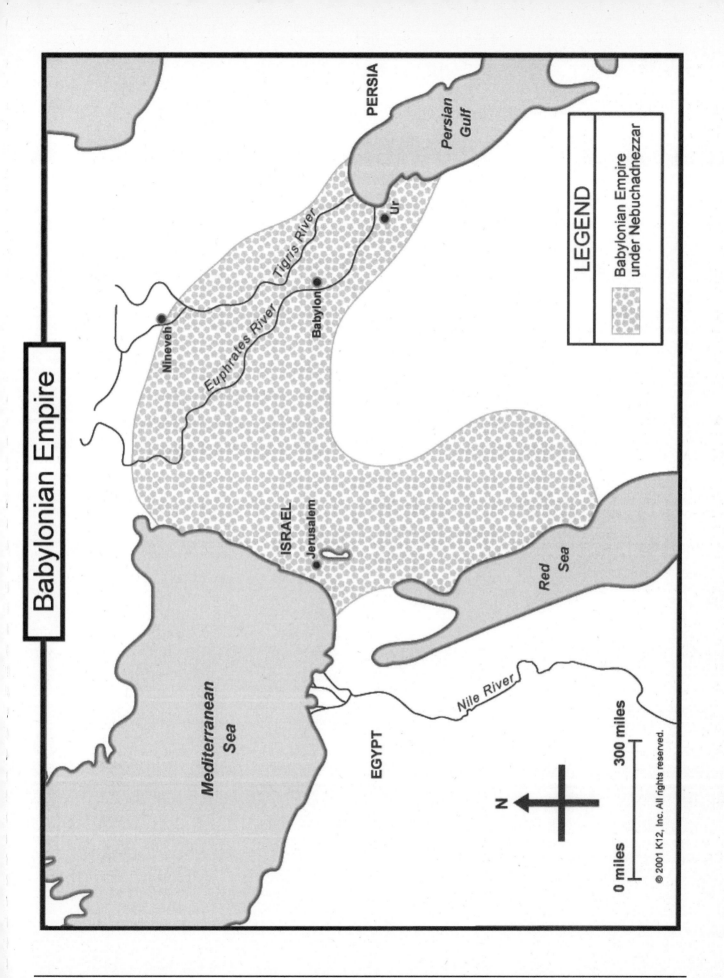

PERSIA

Persian Gulf

Tigris River

Euphrates River

Nineveh

Babylon

Ur

ISRAEL

Jerusalem

Mediterranean Sea

Red Sea

Nile River

EGYPT

LEGEND

Babylonian Empire under Nebuchadnezzar

N

0 miles   300 miles

© 2001 K12, Inc. All rights reserved.

Name _____   Date _____

Ancient Kingdoms Rise and Fall

Select the one best answer. Shade or color the bubble for the answer you choose.

1. To show their power and to make people remember them, pharaohs in ancient Egypt built huge pyramids and temples.
   ○ true
   ○ false

2. An Egyptian woman who became pharaoh was _____.
   ○ Tutankhamen
   ○ Ramses
   ○ Hatshepsut

3. Pharaoh Ramses II is known best for _____.
   ○ building temples and statues
   ○ riding horses and camels
   ○ writing hieroglyphics and cuneiform

4. The Israelite child placed in a basket, discovered by the pharaoh's daughter, and raised as an Egyptian was named _____.
   ○ Joseph
   ○ David
   ○ Moses

5. The Israelites' long journey out of Egypt is called the _____.
   ○ Exodus
   ○ Genesis
   ○ Flight

6. King Solomon was considered a wise king because he _____ .
- ○ was able to solve difficult problems
- ○ knew how to tell exciting stories
- ○ could make good laws

7. The ancient Egyptians believed in many gods. The Israelites believed in
- ○ many gods
- ○ one God
- ○ a sun god and moon god

8. Nebuchadnezzar, a strong king of ancient Babylon, built one of the seven wonders of the ancient world. It was _____ .
- ○ the Pyramids at Giza
- ○ the Ziggurat at Ur
- ○ the Hanging Gardens of Babylon

9. Saul, David, and Solomon were
- ○ the first three kings of the Israelites
- ○ three pharaohs of ancient Egypt
- ○ ancient Mesopotamian warriors

Fill in the blank with the correct answer.

10. The shepherd boy who defeated the giant, Goliath, and later became King of the Israelites was named_____.

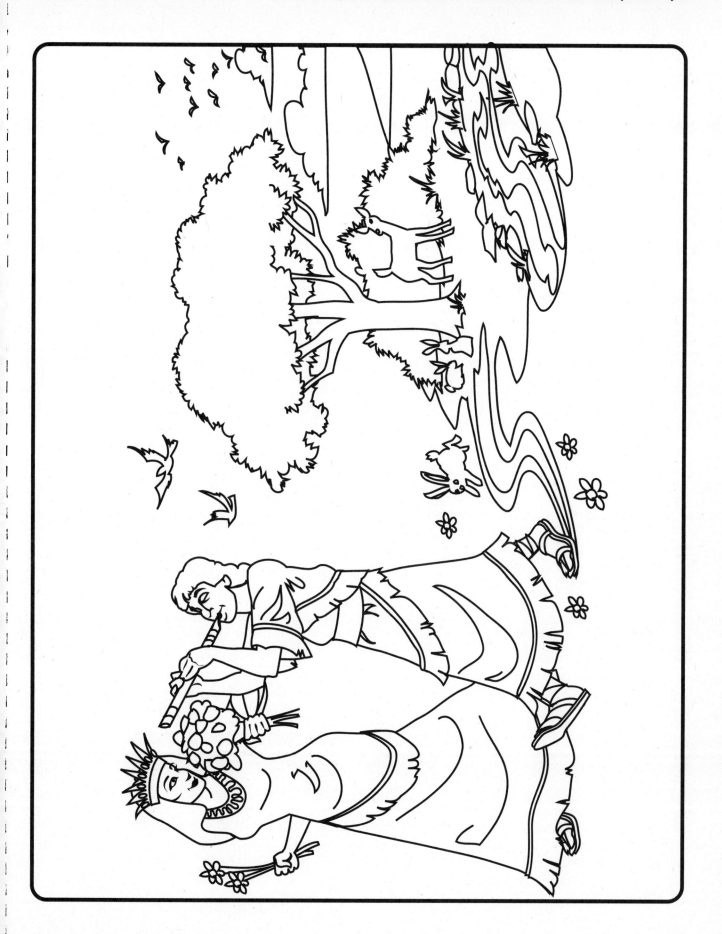

Answer Keys

Lesson Assessment Answer Key

Getting Around the Globe

Answers:

1. continents
2. seven
3. oceans
4. There is much more water than land on Earth
5. Atlantic, Pacific, Indian, or Arctic

Name _____ Date _____

Lesson Assessment Answer Key

Way to Go: Directions

Answers:

1. It helps us find our way around the map.
2. North, South, East, West
3. The student should show an upward direction on the globe
4. The north Pole is on top of the globe, the South Pole is on the bottome of the globe, and the equator is the horizontal line in between them.

Lesson Assessment Answer Key

Our World: The Lay of the Land

Answers:

1. The picture of a glacier was identified.
2. The picture of a mountain was identified.
3. The picture of a desert was identified.
4. The picture of a lake was identified.
5. The picture of an island was identified.
6. The picture of a peninsula was identified.
7. The picture of a canyon was identified.
8. The picture of a river was identified.

Lesson Assessment Answer Key

What is History?

Answers:

1. History
2. Answers may include envelopes, old photographs, a medal, and his grandparents.

Name _____   Date _____

Geography and History Overview: Answer Key

Fill in the blanks with the correct answer.

1. How many continents are there on Earth?   7

2. Is there more land or water on the Earth?   water

3. Place the directions south, east, north, and west in the correct locations on the compass rose.

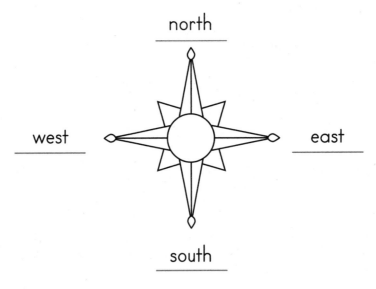

north

west   east

south

Shade or color in the bubble next to the correct answer.

4. Africa and Asia are both _____ .

   ○ islands

   ● continents

   ○ peninsulas

5. Large bodies of water, like the Atlantic and Pacific, are _____.

- ● oceans
- ○ lakes
- ○ rivers

6. A lake is a body of water surrounded by _____.

- ○ mountains
- ○ ice
- ● land

7. Name a dry, sandy place where it's hard for plants and animals to live:

- ○ mountain
- ● desert
- ○ glacier

8. Canyons look like _____.

- ● deep cracks in the earth
- ○ big chunks of ice
- ○ small pools of water

9. The story of the human past is called _____.

- ○ geography
- ● history
- ○ science

10. Who studies the past by digging up the objects people of the past have left behind?

- ● archaeologists
- ○ doctors
- ○ map-makers

Lesson Assessment Answer Key

Nomads: Wandering Families

Answers:

1. People who moved around (wandered) and didn't settle or stay in one place. They moved to gather food from the land around them.
2. roots dug out of the ground; nuts and berries from bushes and trees
3. elk, deer, bison, and wild horses
4. because they hunted all the animals and ate all the plants in one place and had to move to another place to find food
5. caves or tents (and sometimes outside)

Name _____   Date _____

Lesson Assessment Answer Key

Nomads Settle in the Fertile Crescent

Answers:

1. The Fertile Crescent
2. They found food and water. Accept answers such as a river, animals to hunt, nuts, and berries.

Lesson Assessment Answer Key

The First Villages

Answers:

1. the nomads who settled in the Fertile Crescent; early farmers
2. They dug canals from the river and built shadufs.
3. because they kept their own tame animals

Lesson Assessment Answer Key

Egyptians Lived Along the Nile River

Answers:

1. The Nile River runs past the cities of Giza, Memphis, and Thebes.
2. The Egyptian empire runs along the Nile River.
3. rich soil (silt)

Lesson Assessment Answer Key

Gods of Ancient Egypt

Answers:

1. They worshipped many gods and goddesses.
2. Egyptians thought the gods controlled nature.
3. the Sun
4. Osiris

Name _____   Date _____

Lesson Assessment Answer Key

Hieroglyphs

Answers:

1. Hieroglyphs
2. Accept any reasonable answer, for example: To send letters, to tell stories, to make lists, to write down important things that have happened so people in other places and times can know them.

Lesson Assessment Answer Key

Mummies

Answers:

1. so that dead people could go on to live in the next world, the life after death
2. things they believed a dead person would need in the afterlife, such as furniture, jewels, even mummified pets

Lesson Assessment Answer Key

The Great Pyramid

Answers:

1. pyramids
2. Ancient Egyptians built pyramids by hand.
3.

Lesson Assessment Answer Key

Tutankhamen – King Tut

Answers:

1. He was an Egyptian pharaoh.
2. Unlike most other tombs, Tutankhamen's tomb had not been robbed.
3. a golden coffin, a golden mask, a throne, and so on

Name _____   Date _____

Early Civilizations: Answer Key

For questions 1 - 9, read each question out loud. Then read each answer. Fill in the bubble next to the correct answer. For question 10, complete the map activity.

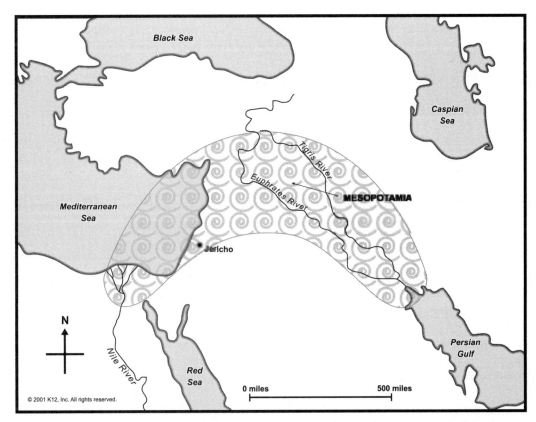

1. Mesopotamian nomads settled in the area shown on the map. What is this area called?

   ○ the desert

   ● the Fertile Crescent

   ○ the Nile River Valley

2. Did ancient Egyptians and Mesopotamians worship one god or many gods?

   ○ one

   ● many

3. Who built the pyramids?
   - ○ Mesopotamians
   - ● Egyptians
   - ○ Nomads

4. Why did the ancient Egyptians preserve the bodies of the dead?
   - ○ So they could display them in museums where millions of people could see them.
   - ● They believed people went on to live in another world and would need their bodies.
   - ○ They wanted their family members to be able to recognize them always.

5. What is ancient Egyptian writing called?
   - ● hieroglyphs
   - ○ cuneiform
   - ○ cursive

6. What did the Nile River do every year?
   - ○ It dried up.
   - ○ It froze into solid ice.
   - ● It flooded and left behind rich soil.

7. What was the ruler of ancient Egypt called?
   - ● pharaoh
   - ○ king
   - ○ prince

8. The civilizations of ancient Egypt and Mesopotamia began near

_____.

- ● rivers
- ○ roads
- ○ mountains

9. What does *Mesopotamia* mean?
- ○ between the mountains
- ● between the rivers
- ○ between the villages

10. Draw a circle around the Nile River on the map below.

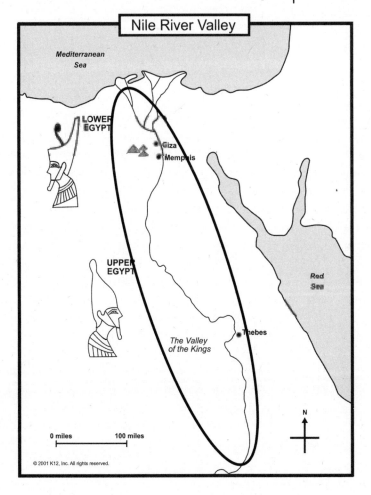

Lesson Assessment Answer Key

Pyramids and Ziggurats

Answers:

1. ziggurats
2. Monuments such as pyramids and ziggurats were built to honor the gods worshipped by people in ancient civilizations.
3.

Name _____ Date _____

Lesson Assessment Answer Key

Abraham Goes to Canaan

Answers:

1. God told him to move.
2. Judaism
3. one god

Lesson Assessment Answer Key

Joseph and the Coat of Many Colors

Answers:

1. the Israelites, or the Jewish people

Lesson Assessment Answer Key

The Israelites Go to Egypt

Answers:

1. Joseph
2. one
3. Canaan

Lesson Assessment Answer Key

The Tower of Babel

Answers:

1. It was a big, powerful city
2. in Mesopotamia
3. ziggurats
4. He made them all speak in different languages.

Lesson Assessment Answer Key

Hammurabi, The Fair King

Answers:

1. laws
2. The Code of Hammurabi
3. No, these were the first known laws.
4. Accept any reasonable answer, for example: To protect people, to be fair, to make sure that leaders do not mistreat people.

Lesson Assessment Answer Key

A Mesopotamian Myth: The Legend of Gilgamesh

Answers:

1. Main events include but are not limited to: Anu sent Enkidu to fight Gilgamesh; Gilgamesh had a dream; a boy befriended Enkidu and taught him to talk, eat and wear clothes; Enkidu and friends went to a wedding in the city; Gilgamesh and Enkidu had a fight; they became friends

Name _____   Date _____

The Rise of Ancient Empires: Answer Key

Select the one best answer. Shade or color the bubble for the answer you choose.

1. Tall, stair-stepped monuments in ancient Mesopotamia are called

   _____.

   ○ pyramids

   ● ziggurats

   ○ cuneiform

2. Egyptian pyramids and Mesopotamian ziggurats show that these ancient

   peoples were good at _____.

   ○ singing

   ● building

   ○ poetry

3. I lived in Ur and traveled to Canaan. God told me to go there and worship

   only one God, not the many gods of Mesopotamia. Who am I?

   ● Abraham

   ○ Sargon

   ○ Joseph

4. Abraham's descendents are called _____.

   ○ Egyptians

   ● Jews

   ○ Babylonians

5. Where did the Israelites go when they left Canaan?
   ○ Mesopotamia
   ○ Babylon
   ● Egypt

6. Babylon was a large, powerful city in _____.
   ● Mesopotamia
   ○ Egypt
   ○ Canaan

7. Hammurabi was famous for writing _____.
   ○ a book of poetry
   ○ a story of gods
   ● a code of laws

8. Followers of Judaism believe in one God.
   ● True
   ○ False

9. I am a king of ancient Mesopotamia who was taught a lesson by a monster named Enkidu. Who am I?
   ○ Hammurabi
   ● Gilgamesh
   ○ Abraham

Locate the following on the map of Mesopotamia.

10. Color Mesopotamia yellow.

11. Draw a red line for the Tigris River.

12. Draw a blue line for the Euphrates River.

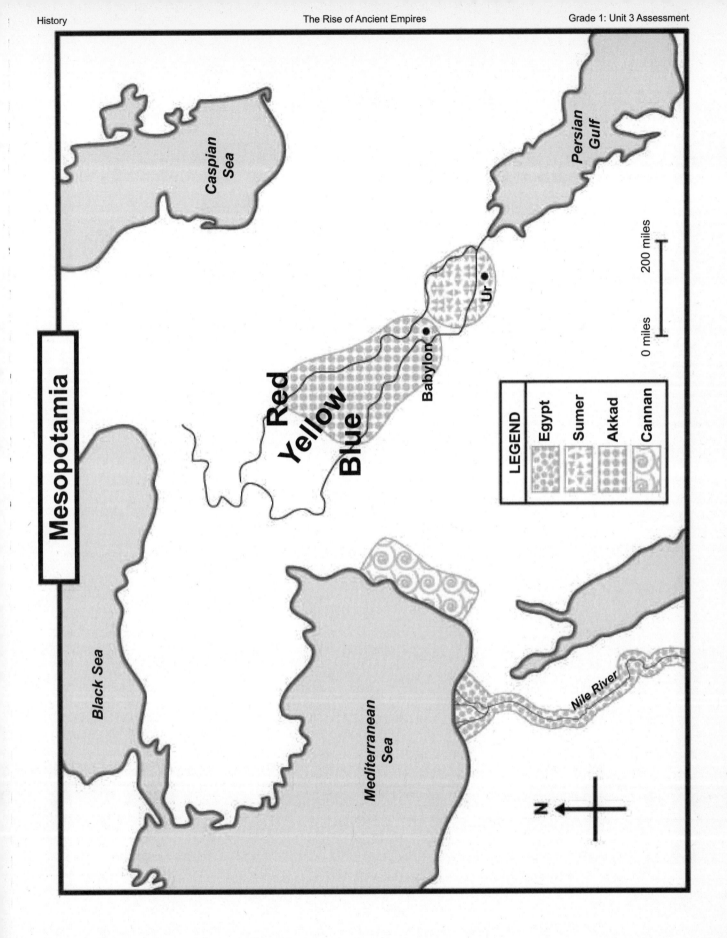

Lesson Assessment Answer Key

A Woman as Pharaoh!

Answers:

1. Hatshepsut
2. The hieroglyphs on the walls of the temple tell us what happened.

Lesson Assessment Answer Key

Ramses II: The Great Builder

Answers:

1. Ramses II
2. Abu Simbel

Lesson Assessment Answer Key

Moses in the Basket

Answers:

1. one
2. because of a famine in Canaan
3. they became slaves
4. Moses

Lesson Assessment Answer Key

The Exodus from Egypt

Answers:

1. Moses
2. the Exodus

Lesson Assessment Answer Key

David, Israel's Second King

Answers:

1. Saul
2. Canaan
3. Answers may vary but should include a combination of: David was a young shepherd boy, an Israelite, they were fighting the Philistine army, Goliath was a giant warrior of the Philistine army, the two fought each other, David used just a sling and was laughed at, but David won.

Lesson Assessment Answer Key

Solomon, the Wise King

Answers:

1. Solomon
2. Answer may include one of the following: think clearly, solve difficult problems, or make good decisions.

Lesson Assessment Answer Key

Back to Babylon

Answers:

1. A strong king of ancient Babylon.
2. the Hanging Gardens of Babylon
3. the Pyramids of Egypt and the Hanging Gardens of Babylon

Name _____   Date _____

Ancient Kingdoms Rise and Fall: Answer Key

Select the one best answer. Shade or color the bubble for the answer you choose.

1. To show their power and to make people remember them, pharaohs in ancient Egypt built huge pyramids and temples.
   - ● true
   - ○ false

2. An Egyptian woman who became pharaoh was _____.
   - ○ Tutankhamen
   - ○ Ramses
   - ● Hatshepsut

3. Pharaoh Ramses II is known best for _____.
   - ● building temples and statues
   - ○ riding horses and camels
   - ○ writing hieroglyphics and cuneiform

4. The Israelite child placed in a basket, discovered by the pharaoh's daughter, and raised as an Egyptian was named _____.
   - ○ Joseph
   - ○ David
   - ● Moses

5. The Israelites' long journey out of Egypt is called the _____.
   - ● Exodus
   - ○ Genesis
   - ○ Flight

6. King Solomon was considered a wise king because he _____ .
   - ● was able to solve difficult problems
   - ○ knew how to tell exciting stories
   - ○ could make good laws

7. The ancient Egyptians believed in many gods. The Israelites believed in
   - ○ many gods
   - ● one God
   - ○ a sun god and moon god

8. Nebuchadnezzar, a strong king of ancient Babylon, built one of the
   seven wonders of the ancient world. It was _____ .
   - ○ the Pyramids at Giza
   - ○ the Ziggurat at Ur
   - ● the Hanging Gardens of Babylon

9. Saul, David, and Solomon were
   - ● the first three kings of the Israelites
   - ○ three pharaohs of ancient Egypt
   - ○ ancient Mesopotamian warriors

Fill in the blank with the correct answer.

10. The shepherd boy who defeated the giant, Goliath, and later
    became King of the Israelites was named_____David_____ .